David's Autobiography

"The Lord has sought out a

man after his own heart

and appointed him

leader of his people"

(1 Samuel 13:14)

Larry D. Rowland

Instant Publishers, Inc.

All Scripture quotations, unless otherwise indicated, are
taken from the New International Version of the Bible.

ISBN: 978-1-60458-646-6

Printed in the United States of America

Table of Contents

Preface

This book is not an autobiography in the literal sense of the word. David, son of Jesse, has been in heaven for almost three thousand years now. And while he was here on this earth, although he was a prolific writer, he never composed a systematized autobiography to our knowledge. In fact, autobiographies, as we know them today, were not commonly written until Augustine composed his famous *Confessions* four hundred years after Jesus Christ walked this earth. So King David probably wouldn't even have considered writing such a book.

But there is a sense in which *Autobiography* is an apt title for this book. David composed much poetry. Poetry, by its very nature, allows the writer's nature and personality to flow through the pen to the parchment. Poetry is the best literary genre to express inner thoughts and feelings. So we are able to learn a great deal more about David as a person through the voluminous poetry that he composed.

This book is an attempt to see how David viewed himself and to discover some of the lessons that he learned in life through his own poetic writings. Selected Davidic Psalms have been chosen representing various periods in the life of this man who is called *a man after God's heart.* As David matured from a shepherd boy to an ambitious teenager to a runaway fugitive to a newly anointed king to a successful conqueror of nations to a capable ruler to a proud abuser of power to a struggling patriarch trying to hold his family together to a legend in his own time, we will see many strategic lessons that he learned as he grew as a person and king.

The Psalms that will form the chapters of this book will not be taken in the order that they are found in the Bible, but will rather be taken chronologically, as they were written in David's life. In this way, we will see David's growth and development from his own perspective. So I invite you to look with me at the greatest of Israel's kings and the founder of the Messianic dynasty.

A MAN AFTER GOD'S OWN HEART
Chapter 1

Henry VIII, the king of England, was in a difficult
situation. He was in the midst of a disagreement with the
Pope that disturbed him greatly. Yes, it was certainly true
that Henry had gotten himself into this mess. Henry had
married Princess Catherine from Spain. As Catherine was
now in her forties and they were yet to have any children,
Henry had begun to panic. He was desperate for an heir to
the English throne. So Henry appealed to the Pope in 1527
for an annulment of his marriage with Catherine so that he
could marry the younger Anne Boleyn. The Pope, surely
pressured by the king of Spain, refused Henry's request for
an annulment. So Henry just divorced Catherine anyway
and married Anne as he had already planned to do. In
retaliation for this obvious snub, the Pope, excommuni-
cated King Henry from the Roman Catholic Church. Now
Henry was a very religious man. This excommunication
distressed him greatly. So the King decided to send one of
his loyal and respected subjects as an emissary to the Pope
in an attempt to patch up this breech in relationship.

The Earl of Wiltshire was chosen for this important
mission. So he with a royal entourage left England to
journey to the Vatican. The Earl also brought his dog who
was his constant and close companion with him. This
move would prove to have disastrous consequences. You
see, everything went along fine at first. The Pope was
pleased with Henry's overture and received the Earl of
Wiltshire graciously. And the Earl quickly fell to his knees
to kiss the toe of the Pope as was the custom when
meeting the Pontiff. But when Pope Clement VII thrust
out his foot towards the Earl, the dog misinterpreted the
action as one of aggression. The Earl's dog jumped

forward and bit the Pope's foot. One of the guards who was always by the Pope's side sprung into action to defend the Pope and immediately killed the dog. Well, the Earl of Wiltshire was crushed and angered at having lost his favorite companion, and he stormed out of the Vatican and back to England, sealing the rift between King Henry and Pope Clement. Within a short period of time, the Church of England was born.

Now most history books contain a chapter on King Henry VIII and his leading England religiously away from the Roman Catholic Church to the formation of the Church of England. Many reasons are usually offered for the split. Among these most often are his marriage, family, and financial pressures. Even Henry's personal character and arrogance are sometimes offered. But seldom is the Earl's dog mentioned. Yet at this most critical moment when reconciliation appeared to be close at hand, it was a dog's mistake and a man's love for his animal that actually helped to redirect English history.

We are all aware of the bond that can grow between a person and a pet animal. Many have a close relationship and affection for a dog or a cat or some other animal. Our much-loved German Shepherd, Bach, was certainly considered to be a member of the Rowland household until he passed away at an old age. Animals can be loyal and constant companions. And animals can help humans learn a lot about themselves and life in general.

It is not happenstance that God chose to prepare David for a lifetime of leading people by giving him the job of herding sheep for the majority of his childhood. God had already used this methodology with great success. God trained Moses by giving him the job of herding sheep out in the wilderness for forty years before he was called

10

to lead the children of Israel out of Egypt. And God chose a similar pattern for David as well. David spent the greater part of his childhood days shepherding the family flocks.

Now there certainly were many disadvantages to being a shepherd in David's day. It could be about the most boring job in the world. It was monotonous. It was mundane. There was nothing to do most of the time. All the shepherd basically did was sit around looking after sheep. It was no wonder that nomadic shepherds had a reputation for being lazy and even dishonest. An ancient Rabbi named Bar Hamma said *there is no more contemptible office in Israel than that of the shepherd.* So it was a humbling experience being chosen to watch the family flocks; it was as if you weren't good enough for any other job.

But there were also some great advantages and opportunities found in being a shepherd. A shepherd had a great deal of time on his hands with nothing much to do. He could either become very lazy and undisciplined or he could become extremely proficient in certain fields if he disciplined himself. David took advantage of the opportunity given to him by developing self-discipline.

Instead of sitting around doing nothing, David made himself a musical instrument and began to practice hour after hour until he became one of the most skilled musicians in the entire country. When King Saul was having one of his severe emotional depressions and a musician was needed to calm his spirit and soothe his soul, David the shepherd was summoned. Out of all the musicians in the entire country, a shepherd was chosen because he had developed unusual skill as a musician. Every musician knows that those kinds of skills come only through hundreds of hours of practice.

Instead of sitting around wasting his time, when he got tired of playing his harp, David set up targets on the stones and practiced hitting them with his sling until he became one of the premiere marksmen in the entire country. He had such confidence that he alone was willing to face the giant, Goliath, when every other soldier shrunk back in fear. David had confidence in his abilities with the sling. This kind of confidence only comes after hours and hours of practice. David was so proficient that he was able to hit a couple of inch square area on Goliath's forehead while on the dead run.

Now you might have been called by God to perform a rather menial task. Your work might be boring and tedious. And it might be true that most of the people that you work with are undisciplined people with severe character deficiencies. They might have given into the desires of the flesh as evidenced by the magazines that they constantly read or the pictures that surround them on the workplace wall. They might have let their minds go as evidenced by their limited vocabulary or the profanity that they constantly use. But the next time you are tempted to be overcome by boredom just think of David's example. A mundane job gives many opportunities to the worker. If you develop your self-discipline, just think of all you could accomplish. Just think of all the Scripture you could memorize. Just think of all the languages you could learn. David became the most skilled musician and marksman in all of Israel, not while playing in the Jerusalem philharmonic orchestra or studying at the Israel military academy, but out on the hillside watching sheep.

Now we don't know exactly when David wrote Psalm 23 in his life, but we can be sure that this Psalm reflects spiritual lessons that he learned during his childhood because this was the only time when he was active in herding sheep. And it is clear from this autobiographical statement of his spiritual life that David was a man who had a special relationship with the Lord. But his was a relationship that each of us can have for God desires for all of us, as members of his flock, to know Him as our Shepherd.

There are many different ways to look at Psalm 23. There are many commentaries on this familiar passage. Those written by Leupold, Alexander and Kidner are three of my favorites. Philip Keller has an excellent little book looking at this passage from a cultural point of view. But one can also try to look at this Psalm through David's eyes. This approach reveals three spiritual lessons that David learned as a shepherd.

David first learned **to rely upon the Lord** for all of his physical, emotional and spiritual needs in life.

The LORD is my shepherd; I shall not be in want. He makes me lie down in green pastures, he leads me beside quiet waters, he restores my soul. He guides me in paths of righteousness for his name's sake. (Psalm 23:1-3)

David began this Psalm by speaking of the Lord who met all his needs so that he had no wants. He pointed out specific needs that the Lord meets:

*He gives physical nourishment and contentment by making him to lie down in green pastures.

*He gives life-giving refreshment by leading him besides the quiet waters.

*He gives emotional strength and stability by restoring his soul.

*He gives spiritual direction by guiding him in paths of righteousness.

In short, David was willing to admit that he was a needy person. And he learned that the Lord was able and willing to meet all of those needs in their fullness so that he wouldn't be in want in any area of his life. This, very simply, is one of the most important lessons that people can ever learn in their relationships with the Lord.

Now we might think this to be such an obvious lesson, but it is one that is so difficult for us to learn. For part of the core of our sinful human natures is a strong desire to be self-sufficient, totally independent of anyone or anything outside of ourselves. Every person has a strong inner desire to be in ultimate control of his or her life.

This innate desire is seen in the heroes that we have invented. Just think for a moment of the fantasy heroes that have been invented and accepted by our youth. When I was young, Superman sold the most comic books and had a regular series on the television. I have noticed that he regularly makes comebacks with every generation. Superman has endured the test of time as an American cultural hero. What is it that makes Superman so appealing to us? He is self-sufficient, isn't he? He has powers and abilities to defend himself and he even can save the world all by himself. Superman doesn't need God. You have never seen him pray. He doesn't need to pray. He can do whatever is needed to sustain life by himself. And most of us growing up entertain this same fantasy in our minds. We all have the desire for self-sufficiency, and this innate desire can keep us from having the relationship with God that is available to us, the relationship that David had.

The reality is that there isn't another mammal born on this planet that is in a more helpless condition than the human baby. There are some animals born that can scavenge for food immediately; not so with a human baby who is totally dependent upon the mother's milk. There are some animals born that can get up and walk almost immediately; not so with a human baby who must be carried around by a parent. There are some animals born that can function rather independently soon after birth; not so with the human baby who cannot even think rationally until months after birth. And this dependency that is realized at birth is just typical of the kind of dependency that we have on God throughout our entire lifetimes. We don't want it; we didn't vote for it; we often resent it; but it is fact. It is reality. We are dependent upon God for every heartbeat and breath for our entire lifetime. The One who gave life to us at conception is also the One who sustains that life until he gives to us our final breath. And the quicker we come to grips with this reality in life, the better off we are. For accepting the frailty of our human condition releases us to find all of our needs met in the Lord who desires to be our Shepherd.

Now David learned this great lesson as a youth shepherding his father's flocks. A sheep left to itself in Israel would quickly die. It either would be consumed by hungry predators (sheep are totally defenseless animals slowed down by heavy coats of wool) or it would starve to death. It is absolutely necessary for flocks to follow migratory patterns in Israel to obtain sufficient nourishment. Sheep, by emitting a unique odor from their hooves, have a tendency to go back to the same location to feed day after day for security rather than venturing out to new pastureland. A sheep left totally unattended would also risk dehydration. Sheep have a natural fear of any moving waters and don't want to go near them. Sheep also risk being controlled and dominated by parasites for sheep are natural harbors for all kinds of parasitic animals and are totally defenseless against them. The nasal fly, for instance, will come and lay eggs in the moist recesses of a sheep's nose. When the eggs hatch, the maggots that crawl around cause such irritation that sheep will literally beat themselves senseless smashing their heads against trees or rocks unless that parasite is controlled.

David knew all this. He took care of sheep for years. He fought the bear and the lion that were trying to prey on his helpless sheep. He knew the migratory patterns that Jewish shepherds must follow in order to provide adequate pastureland for their flocks. He knew where the pools of water were where the sheep would drink without fear of drowning. He undoubtedly had his own special recipe of oil, sulfur and tar that he would use to rub on his sheep's head to ward off the dreaded nasal fly. And somewhere along the way, as David was caring for the family flocks, the truth dawned on him that in God's eyes, he was like one of these sheep. He realized that God looked upon him in the same way he looked upon one of the members of his flock. He was just as dependent upon God as his sheep were dependent upon him. This was a tremendously freeing truth for David. For it both allowed him to see life as it really was, and it also put him into a position where God was able to release his strength and power into David's life in a special way.

You see, as long as a person is convinced that he can live life in his own strength and is committed to trying it, God must just stand back and watch him fail. For the one thing that God will not do is give his glory to another. If God gave the self-sufficient person his omnipotent power, that person would claim credit for it. That person would claim to be a superman. But when a person admits inadequacies and weaknesses and comes to God

16

requesting divine strength and power, God is always ready and willing to come to that person's aid. It is so important to learn to rely upon the Lord for all of our physical, emotional and spiritual needs.

There is a second lesson that David learned that is revealed in this Psalm. David learned **to trust in the Lord** when he had anxieties and fears in life.

Even though I walk through the valley of the shadow of death, I will fear no evil, for you are with me; your rod and your staff, they comfort me. (Psalm 23:4)

Now this passage is often used in the context of facing death. In fact, I myself have often used this passage when delivering funeral eulogies in my pastoral ministry. Many times, Psalm 23 is the passage requested by the family for it is such a beloved and well-known text. And this verse does have an application concerning death and the courage that a person can have in facing death if he or she is following the Lord as shepherd.

But the primary interpretation of Psalm 23:4 is not found in facing the natural death that is common to all. The valley of the shadow of death was the name of a road in ancient times. It was the name of the road that joined the cities of Jerusalem and Jericho. It was the very road that the Jewish man was walking down when he was robbed by a thief and then rescued by the Good Samaritan in Christ's story. The city of Jerusalem has an elevation of about twenty-five hundred feet above sea level. Jericho is near the northern border of the Dead Sea which is below sea level. The Valley of the Shadow of Death was the road between Jerusalem and Jericho that fell a couple thousand feet in about forty miles. It was a road that often had treacherous footing, was very circuitous, and had steep cliffs and crevices alongside it. It was a natural place for bandits to lurk. There were plenty of hiding places. And it could be especially lucrative when the pilgrims came to Jerusalem during the special feast days carrying large sums of monies for offerings and sacrifices. That is one of the reasons for pilgrims travelling in large groups, for protection as well as for company.

The point that David was making here reflected the migratory patterns of nomadic shepherding. The conscientious shepherd had to move his flocks from the higher elevations of summer to the lower elevations in the winter. The most natural routes would be through the valleys that had the gentlest slopes and were the best watered. But there were many dangers lurking in these valleys for the sheep. There were the predators that were always ready to prey upon the helpless; there was poor footing that could lead to stumbles along the way; there were steep crevices that could quickly end one's life. The sheep would naturally be fearful of making such a journey even though it was for their wellbeing to introduce them to better pastureland on the other side. But as long as they were with the shepherd, they needn't have fear for their shepherd would guide and protect them. Even if they had to journey down that most dreaded road, the valley of the shadow of death, they needn't fear if their shepherd were with them.

David was a man who knew the nature of fear. He knew the clutching grip of terror. In later chapters, we will see some Psalms that were written as he was fleeing for his life from Saul. David was a man who knew the realities of life's dangers personally. But somewhere along life's journey, David also learned the comfort of having the Lord as his shepherd. So David learned to place his life in the hands of the Lord. This freed him from anxiety and fear.

This allowed his mind to think swiftly and logically in an emergency. David was not a man who was paralyzed by fear. He was a man who was at his very best when under pressure. David was able to function in this way because he knew the Lord as one who could free him from anxiety and fears. How many people are hindered in reaching their life's potential by fear? All of us wrestle with our anxieties to some extent. But many are actually stymied and paralyzed by their anxieties and fears. Yes, there are many dangers in this life and they are real and foreboding. But if we know the Lord as our Shepherd, and if we are walking with Him in fellowship, we can even walk through the valley of the shadow of death with confidence.

A third lesson that David learned as revealed in this Psalm was his **hope in the Lord** for what lay ahead in the future.

You prepare a table before me in the presence of my enemies. You anoint my head with oil; my cup overflows. Surely goodness and love will follow me all the days of my life, and I will dwell in the house of the LORD forever. (Psalm 23:5,6)

How many details of his future did David actually know at the time of his writing? We can't be sure. Did he know of the decade of his life that would be spent running from the sword of Saul? Did he know of all of the battles that he would have to fight in order to deliver the Israelites from the dominance of surrounding nations? Did he know of the internal battles that he would have to suffer with his own sinful flesh and depraved desires? Did he realize that members of his very family, his own flesh and blood, would one day rise up against him in an attempt to take his throne and life? We don't know how much David knew when he wrote these words. But we do know that David knew the Lord as his Shepherd. And knowing the Lord as his shepherd gave confidence to him to face the future with hope. David knew that goodness and mercy would follow him all the days of his life because he had confidence in the Lord as his shepherd. And I'm sure that just as David might not have known all of the trials that lay ahead of him in life, he surely didn't have any idea of the glories that were in store for him either. Could he in his wildest imagination have dreamed of the honor and glory that he would experience being the king of Israel? Do you think he would have ever guessed how easily the Philistines would be subdued after decades of domination over Israel? Could David's mind have ever conceived of the riches that he would accumulate in his lifetime having enough left over to provide for the glorious temple of God? Do you think that David ever envisioned the palace that he would live in one day as he slept out under the stars on those barren hillsides with his sheep? No, at this point in his life, I'm sure that David never envisioned all of the glories that lay ahead for him. But because he knew the Lord as his Shepherd, he could face the future with absolute confidence.

And far greater than the prospect of having goodness and love follow him all the days of his earthly life, David had the confidence that he would one day dwell in the house of the Lord forever. That assurance alone makes all the trials and struggles of this life bearable.

FLEE LIKE A BIRD
Chapter 2

Steve Richardson is regarded as one of the premiere puzzle-makers of all time. Steve left an accounting firm in New Jersey to join a small computer company in the smaller town of Hanover, New Hampshire. Six months later Steve was laid off, unemployed. Steve then decided to join with a friend in doing what he wanted to do most - making jig saw puzzles. *Steve Puzzles, Inc.* was born.

Steve's goal is simple. *I want to make a puzzle that's possible to do but that nobody can do.* The puzzles that Steve produces are not inexpensive ranging from about a hundred to over seven thousand dollars. But each puzzle is uniquely handmade. Most are composed of an original art print bonded to some plywood backing. Then the puzzle is cut by an electric jigsaw with a blade about as thin as the hair of a horse's tail. Steve's puzzles have found their way into Queen Elizabeth's palace and the White House. George and Laura Bush were big fans of Steve's puzzles.

Many of the puzzles are novel. There is one, for instance, that is made entirely out of chocolate. (I wonder how long that one would last around our house.) Another one is so small that it comes with tweezers. One of Steve's favorite is called *The Three Little Pigs*. The pieces fit together sixty-three wrong ways and only one right way. A twenty-six year old administrator from Texas requested a special puzzle for his girlfriend. As she assembled it, she discovered a Victorian Bride putting her veil on for her wedding. Only when the puzzle was completed did the message appear: *Will You Marry Me?*

But of all the puzzles that Steve Richardson has designed, there is only one that was a complete failure. A couple of years ago, he designed an April Fool's Day Puzzle called *Five Easy Pieces.* It was a joke. No matter how a person put it together, one piece always wouldn't fit. Steve's customers didn't think it was funny. After demanding the solution, all of them asked for their money back. *I had to buy back all thirty of those puzzles,* Steve recalled glumly in an interview. The people just couldn't stand to have a puzzle that couldn't be completed, a puzzle that wouldn't fit together properly.

There is something within us that desires everything to fit together properly. I am sure that if a psychological study were done of jig saw puzzle enthusiasts, a major attraction of the puzzles would be the satisfaction found at the completion when all the pieces fit together perfectly. There is nothing quite as irritating as coming across an old puzzle in a box, perhaps bought at a garage sale, spending the time putting it all together, and finding out in the end that there was just one piece that was lost. We like to have completion in life, don't we? Completion brings order and stability to our lives.

This inner longing that we have is the reason for our distress and frustration when those elements of life that we consider to be foundational begin to fall apart on us. When we have family struggles or breakups, when churches split, when the economy plunges into recession, when there is a major scandal that is uncovered in some government office, we are deeply bothered and affected. It is as if a piece to our life puzzle has been lost and we long for it to be found and put back into place again.

David went through a rather lengthy period of his young life when the world seemed to be falling apart around him. But it was during this very difficult period in

David's life that he learned some invaluable lessons that would give guidance and direction to the entirety of his life.

Few people have ever risen from obscurity to national prominence more quickly than David did. We live in a day when it is not uncommon for an athlete or movie star to become a household name overnight, but that didn't regularly happen back in David's time. There was no television back then. There was no internet. No, the normal course of fame was a long, slow climb through all of the proper channels.

But that is not what happened to David. There were two events during his mid-teenage years that quickly propelled David into the national spotlight. The first was his victory over a Philistine giant named Goliath. We will not dwell on this event long because the story of David and Goliath is well known. A nine foot six inch Philistine named Goliath had intimidated the entire Israeli army. He had come out regularly to challenge any Jewish soldier to a duel. As he stood there with his bronze armor weighing over a hundred pounds and carrying his spear whose point weighed about fifteen pounds, he had the entire army of Saul quaking in fear. David had been sent by his father, Jesse, to give some provisions to his brothers who were in the army when he happened to hear Goliath's boastful challenge. As you probably already know, David accepted that challenge and armed with only a sling and five stones, the teenager killed Goliath, routing the entire Philistine army. David's victory brought a welcome relief from Philistine oppression for just a little while and made the teenager an instant hero in the land. David immediately went from being a shepherd nobody to a soldier hero. Even to this day, when somebody faces immeasurable odds, the story of David and Goliath is often brought up as a source of encouragement and inspiration.

The other factor in David's quick propulsion to fame was necessitated by Saul's emotional problems. King Saul had a severe emotional disorder. He would often plunge into depths of depression. His aides found that music was helpful in soothing his spirit. So David was called upon on a regular basis to play a personal concert on his harp for the King in order to bring tranquility to his troubled soul. David's skill as a musician made him not only a regular personality around the palace, but also a much needed help in maintaining order and in keeping up morale. So it should not be surprising that David's popularity and fame skyrocketed in the nation of Israel.

It is ironic that it was the very help that David gave to Saul that both resulted in his increased popularity and also brought about so much trouble for the teenager. For while Saul needed David so much to soothe his troubled spirit, the King also resented David's popularity and became insanely jealous of him. Interestingly, it was a short song that Saul heard some women singing that was the major source of irritation for him. *Saul has killed his thousands and David his tens of thousands.* After Saul heard the women singing this song, the Bible says that he became very angry and this refrain galled him. (1 Sam. 18:8)

Now one might think that Saul would be pleased to be exalted as a great war hero. After all, the song did praise him as a courageous leader. But all Saul could hear was the greater praise being given to David. This gnawed at his insides.

It has been said that when some people look at a land of milk and honey, they can only see cholesterol and calories. Sadly, this is what happened with Saul. Instead of being pleased with the praise being given to him, he became insanely jealous of David and began looking for a way to kill this person who was his greatest asset in ruling his kingdom.

The situation became very tense for David when Saul's anger and jealousy boiled over into overt action. Several times, Saul hurled his spear at David while he was playing his harp at the palace. Each time, David managed to escape in a miraculous way. But it was clear to everyone that David's life was in great danger. It was probably during this period of time, when David was trying to maintain his loyalty to King Saul as court musician in a most dangerous situation, that Psalm 11 was written. These brief seven verses tell volumes about the inner struggles that David was enduring.

In the LORD I take refuge. How then can you say to me: "Flee like a bird to your mountain. For look, the wicked bend their bows; they set their arrows against the strings to shoot from the shadows at the upright in heart. When the foundations are being destroyed, what can the righteous do?"
The LORD is in his holy temple; the LORD is on his heavenly throne. He observes the sons of men; his eyes examine them. The LORD examines the righteous, but the wicked and those who love violence his soul hates. On the wicked he will rain fiery coals and burning sulfur; a scorching wind will be their lot. For the LORD is righteous, he loves justice; upright men will see his face. (Psalm 11)

Close friends were warning David to get away from the palace while he still could. They feared for his life. *Flee like a bird to your mountain,* they were advising him as David admits in the first verses. Run, David, run. Get away while you still can. But David was hesitant to go. Perhaps he just didn't want to believe that Saul really wanted to kill him after all that he had done for the king. But probably it was even more than this. David's world was falling apart. He had come to the palace as a teenager with high hopes and ideals. Up to this time, he had only heard about the glories of the palace as a shepherd boy. Now he had experienced them personally. But he didn't find what he thought he would. Instead of a regal, courageous monarch he had found a raving lunatic. It is likely that David just didn't want to face the reality of his disillusionment. He didn't want to admit the fact that his life and the lives of his family members were in serious danger. He didn't want to face the fact that so much of what had been foundational in his life was just crumbling under him at such a young age. *When the foundations are being destroyed, what can the righteous do?* David asks mournfully in Ps. 11:3.

What does a person do when the foundations in life are crumbling? When a person receives word that his factory is shutting down and he is going to lose his job, what does he do? When the family is struggling along, just hanging on by a thread, what does a person do? When a person picks up a paper and reads about seemingly unsolvable problems throughout the world, what can she do? What does a person do when the foundations of life, the institutions that have brought security and stability to life, appear to be crumbling?

David faced these questions and he reveals how he dealt with them in this brief Psalm. What we specifically see as we look at this Psalm are four insights that David had into the person and character of God that allowed him to keep going when it seemed like the foundations were being destroyed.

First of all, David realized that **God had not abdicated his sovereign throne**. The earthly king Saul might be unraveling at the seams, but Almighty God was still seated securely on his throne in heaven.

When the foundations are being destroyed, what can the righteous do?" The LORD is in his holy temple; the LORD is on his heavenly throne. (Psalm 11:3,4a)

Now this insight is very critical for it forms a key to David's being able to cope with his feeling that the foundations were being destroyed. Whenever we feel that the foundations are being destroyed, we also feel that everything is completely out of control. David's friends reveal that kind of panicky feeling. *Flee like a bird to your mountain* was their advice to him. Run for your life, David. Everything is out of control. There is no hope. Just run for it and try to save yourself.

And there are times when we feel the very same way. But it is exactly during these times that we must again realize that God has not abdicated his throne. God hasn't gone anywhere; he is still there. The same God who overturned the mighty Pharaoh, the same God who toppled the walls of Jericho, the same God who raised Jesus Christ victoriously from the grave, that same God is on the throne. He knows what is going on; he is not blind. He is aware of all that is happening; he never slumbers or sleeps. *The Lord is in his holy temple; the Lord is on his heavenly throne.* We must start here with this statement.

Perhaps the greatest president that our country ever had was approached by a concerned citizen during the turbulent times of the Civil War. Our whole country seemed to be falling apart as brother was fighting against brother, and hatred reigned across the land. The citizen asked Abraham Lincoln if he had the confidence that God was on the side of the north in the struggle against the south. President Lincoln's answer showed great wisdom. *My greatest concern, sir, is not whether or not God is on my side, but rather it is whether or not I am on God's side.* A key in Abraham Lincoln maintaining his perspective and balance during the Civil War was his knowledge that God was still on the throne. As long as he remained on God's side, he could have confidence in any direction taken.

But David not only remembered that God was still on his throne, he also realized that his character had not changed. **God remained a righteous God.**

The LORD is in his holy temple; the LORD is on his heavenly throne. He observes the sons of men; his eyes examine them. The LORD examines the righteous, but the wicked and those who love violence his soul hates. (Psalm 11:4,5)

The God in heaven is not an absentee God. He is rather a God who is very interested in the affairs of his creatures. He carefully observes all that they do. He scrutinizes them. He not only looks at the outward actions, but he also has the ability to look at the inward attitudes and motives. God knows the difference between a righteous act, one that is done with sincere and proper motives, and a wicked act, one that is done to hurt someone else or for purely selfish reasons. The word for *righteousness* comes from the root word meaning *straight* in the Bible. Therefore, the righteousness of God simply means that he, by his character, is committed to doing that which is straight, that which is proper, that which is in the loving best interests of his creation, that which is right.

Human standards often change. That which was considered to be unethical or immoral yesterday might be accepted by society today. But God's standards never change. He knows what is right because he is a righteous God. And he is committed to act according to his nature.

A third lesson that David learned through his distress was **God's power to act** in the defense of his people. Because God is righteous in his character, he will defend those who do right and oppose those who do wrong. When we sense the foundations crumbling beneath our feet, we must never underestimate the power of God.

On the wicked he will rain fiery coals and burning sulfur; a scorching wind will be their lot. (Psalm 11:6)

Now one of the major conflicts that we have when we sense foundations crumbling is the injustice of it all. Sometimes it appears that only those who are dishonest or unethical really get ahead in life. Only those who can shade the truth and speak out of both sides of their mouths can be successful politicians. Only those who are the most aggressive in seeking to destroy the stable institutions of our society seem to be rewarded with honor and fame and money. Whatever happened to the honest people of integrity who faithfully perform their duties before God?

We need to remember that God is observing all that is happening here on the earth. And that even when he does not reward righteousness and punish wickedness immediately (as often is the case), there will be a day of reckoning coming. David realized this truth and it allowed him to maintain his integrity in an upside down world.

In 1620, a group of God-fearing people braved the storms of the Atlantic Ocean to come from England to America. We remember them today as the Pilgrims. They never should have survived the trip. The odds were certainly stacked against them, crammed in the belly of that ship all the way across the ocean. There had originally been two ships, but the one failed to pass the safety inspections. So all who had been booked on the two ships were crammed into the Mayflower. They left England at a very poor time for trans-Atlantic travel, but they were desperate people because of the severe persecutions they had suffered. As if the trip itself weren't traumatic enough, there was one salty seaman who was especially wicked and sadistic. He delighted in making fun of these *landlovers* who were not used to sea travel. He would taunt and curse them. He would constantly tell them that they would never make it, that they would all die at sea. And he would always conclude by saying that it was going to be his delight to bury them all at sea. *Fishbait*, that's what you will be, *fishbait*. But God was with those early Pilgrims and he honored their faith and courage. Every single passenger, every man, woman and child survived that voyage. Yes, history records for us that every person aboard the Mayflower survived that sixty-seven day nightmare- that is except for one person. The only one who did not survive was that profane, godless sailor. Just past the halfway point, he fell mysteriously ill with a serious infection, and he died several weeks later in lingering agony. Our pilgrim fathers were convinced that his death was the result of God's justice.

God does not normally execute his judgments in such an immediate fashion. But his mercy and patience do not indicate weakness on his part. David realized this. God's righteous character and his unchanging power gave to him the strength needed during those days when he sensed the foundations crumbling under him.

When a person studies the character of God and realizes his awesome power to judge, a proper fear and respect for such a mighty being is just a natural response. An omnipotent being who is committed by his character to rain fiery coals and burning sulfur on the wicked should strike great apprehension into our hearts. The image that David's words bring to mind is that of Sodom and Gomorrah burning in God's judgment. Perhaps that was the picture that David was seeing when he penned these words.

How happy we are that God has revealed to us the way to become righteous in his sight. It is not through our own feeble attempts at good works. No, the Bible tells us that God's son, Jesus Christ, was made sin for us on the cross of Calvary so that we might be made the righteousness of God in him. (2 Cor. 5:21) God has provided the means for our becoming righteous in his sight. The Son of God became a human so that humans could become children of God. Jesus Christ came to earth and died so that we might be able to attain the character of God through him. David knew that gracious God as well as the God of great wrath and judgment. David knew a God who forgave sins as well as a God of power and justice. And this very God brought to David stability during the times when the foundations seemed to be crumbling all around him.

So then, David answered his own question by remembering that God had not abdicated his throne, that his righteous character had not changed and that he remained a powerful God. The injustice that David was witnessing was not a testimony to God not caring, God changing his standards or God being too weak to stop it. God remained in the heavens the same God as always.

But there was also one more insight that David shared. After reviewing the wonderful character of God, David concluded with **an affirmation of fellowship**.

For the LORD is righteous, he loves justice; upright men will see his face. (Psalm 11:7)

The mental image of his family and the hope that one day he would be united in fellowship with them once again has kept many a prisoner of war alive during the times when all hope appeared to be lost. So it is that the hope of one day being united with the Lord in fellowship forever can keep us faithful in service to the Lord during days when the foundations appear to be crumbling. The righteous person, the upright person will one day see the face of God. And that will make every sacrifice in this life worthwhile.

Every person has periods in life when the foundations seem to be shaking. Every person has times when life seems to be falling apart. David would know just how we feel because he felt the same way. But David, in spite of his feelings, was able to gain strength from the Lord and go on to live a very productive and successful life. He did this by affirming the fact that, even in the midst of the storm, God is still on his throne in heaven. His character and his power remain unchanged. He welcomes the fellowship of his people. He longs to reach down to them in their time of need and give them sustaining strength and grace. And the one who lives the life of the righteous looks forward to eternal fellowship with him in heaven.

THE OPPORTUNIST
Chapter 3

Our country's twenty-eighth President, Woodrow Wilson served in our nation's highest office at a most difficult time in history. During his first term, he was trying to lead our country in walking the tightrope of neutrality while war was raging in Europe. Finally, when our ships were attacked by German submarines and neutrality was no longer possible, President Wilson led our nation to victory in World War 1 in his second term. Then after the war ended, he helped to draft the peace Treaty of Versailles. In addition to all that was happening on the international front, President Wilson administrated our country when we were moving into the modern era. When he assumed the presidency, there were less than five hundred thousand cars on the streets. By the time he finished office, there were over eight million cars on the road. While many are rightly critical of his progressive policies that have led our country to burdensome debt and socialized programs, historians still consider him one of the top five most influential presidents in our country's illustrious history.

One of the characteristics that made Wilson such a leader was his ability to spot those around him who were trying to secure and use political office for personal gain in an opportunistic way. Unlike some other presidents in our history who have been constantly used by people for personal gain, Woodrow Wilson had the discernment to spot the insincere motives of opportunists.

Wilson often told of the time when he first confronted this problem as governor of New Jersey. One of the senators of his state had suddenly and tragically died. The passing of this senator was a shock to then

Governor Wilson and the whole state. But within just a couple of hours of the senator's death, even before any viewing or funeral arrangements had been announced, Wilson received a phone call from an aspiring politician. After a brief word of greeting, the caller said, *let me just get right to the point of my call. I'd like to take the senator's place.* Well, Woodrow Wilson was so taken back by the blatant insensitivity and opportunism of the caller that he didn't even know how to respond at first. But then after a few moments of uncomfortable silence, the thought came to him. *Well,* he finally answered, *I guess that it's all right with me if the funeral director doesn't mind.*

One of the skills that any leader has to hone is the ability to spot the insincere motives of an opportunist person. If any individual is aspiring to a position with purely selfish motives, without a heart to serve others, that person doesn't have a chance to be successful in that position. Especially as the leader of a nation, with many people trying to climb the ladder to personal power, it is critically important for the chief executive to be able to spot opportunism. Recognizing the necessity of this skill in a good leader, it should not surprise us that this was one of the first lessons that God chose to teach David as he was beginning his training to be King of Israel.

David obviously needed to have a great deal of preparation in order to be the kind of king that God desired for him to be. You can learn something about discipline, character and work habits as a shepherd, but you don't learn what you need to know about administration, government protocol or international policies while herding sheep. So David, having graduated from the school of shepherding with his B.A. degree (we might call this the Baaa degree), was now ready to enroll in the school of being a fugitive where he would learn some valuable lessons enabling him to become a great king.

The stresses and pressures in the palace finally became so severe for David that he had to flee for his life. Saul had tried several times to thrust his spear through David while he was playing his musical instrument. The benefit of having delivered the Israelites from the Philistines for a short time by killing Goliath had now seemingly turned into a liability since Saul had become insanely jealous of David's popularity with the people. David had even become fearful of personally returning to the palace. So he arranged with his close friend, Jonathan, to check out the atmosphere and tell him if it was safe to return or not. As Saul's son, Jonathan would have an access into the thought patterns of Saul that nobody else would have. When Jonathan realized that it really was unsafe for David to return and warned him to flee quickly for his life, all of the realities of being a fugitive immediately consumed the mind of David. Now David was a teenager at this time. But he suddenly had all of the pressures of a life and death struggle placed upon his shoulders.

It should not surprise anyone that David made some very rash and unwise decisions at this time in his life. After all, his head was spinning. He didn't know what to do or where to turn. But God used even some of these poor decisions to teach David some very valuable lessons that we will now look at in this and the next few chapters.

An executive of a very large company was once asked for the single key to being a successful CEO. *I can give you that answer in just two words - good decisions,* he answered. *But how does one know how to make good decisions?* the interviewer continued. The CEO replied, *I* can give you that answer in just one word - *experience.* The interviewer was still not satisfied so he followed up with a final question. *But what is the key to getting experience?* The executive concluded, *I can also give you that answer in just two words - bad decisions.*

Most people look at poor decisions that are made in life as horrible failures. And it is certainly true that none of us purposefully chooses to make a bad decision. But if we learn from poor decisions that we have made, we can grow in wisdom and experience and be better qualified to make better decisions in the future.

The first decision that David made as a fugitive was a horrible one. It was one that could have resulted in untold grief and guilt for the rest of his life. David was likely on his own for the first time in his life, accompanied only by a few friends, perhaps a servant or two. He desperately felt the need for some support. So he ran to the Levitical city called Nob in order to obtain support from the priests there. David did not stop long enough to think through the dangerous position that he was subjecting on these priests. David as a scared young man was just thinking of himself and how to save his own life.

The Biblical account that reveals this first decision that David made and the consequences of it is found in the 21st chapter of 1 Samuel. It is critically important to understand this scene for it forms the setting out of which Psalm 52 was written.

David went to Nob, to Ahimelech the priest. Ahimelech trembled when he met him, and asked, "Why are you alone? Why is no one with you?"

David answered Ahimelech the priest, "The king charged me with a certain matter and said to me, `No one is to know anything about your mission and your *instructions.' As for my men, I have told them to meet me at a certain place. Now then, what do you have on hand? Give me five loaves of bread, or whatever you can find."*

But the priest answered David, "I don't have any ordinary bread on hand; however, there is some consecrated bread here--provided the men have kept themselves from women."

David replied, "Indeed women have been kept from us, as usual whenever I set out. The men's things are holy even on missions that are not holy. How much more so today!" So the priest gave him the consecrated bread, since there was no bread there except the bread of the Presence that had been removed from before the LORD and replaced by hot bread on the day it was taken away.

Now one of Saul's servants was there that day, detained before the LORD; he was Doeg the Edomite, Saul's head shepherd. David asked Ahimelech, "Don't you have a spear or a sword here? I haven't brought my sword or any other weapon, because the king's business was urgent."

The priest replied, "The sword of Goliath the Philistine, whom you killed in the Valley of Elah, is here; it is wrapped in a cloth behind the ephod. If you want it, take it; there is no sword here but that one."

David said, "There is none like it; give it to me."
That day David fled from Saul. (1 Samuel 21:1-10a)

The very next chapter in 1 Samuel shows the tragic results of David's coming to the priests at Nob.

Now Saul heard that David and his men had been discovered. And Saul, spear in hand, was seated under the tamarisk tree on the hill at Gibeah, with all his officials standing around him. Saul said to them, "Listen, men of

Benjamin! Will the son of Jesse give all of you fields and vineyards? Will he make all of you commanders of thousands and commanders of hundreds? Is that why you have all conspired against me? No one tells me when my son makes a covenant with the son of Jesse. None of you is concerned about me or tells me that my son has incited my servant to lie in wait for me, as he does today."

But Doeg the Edomite, who was standing with Saul's officials, said, "I saw the son of Jesse come to Ahimelech son of Ahitub at Nob. Ahimelech inquired of the LORD for him; he also gave him provisions and the sword of Goliath the Philistine."

Then the king sent for the priest Ahimelech son of Ahitub and his father's whole family, who were the priests at Nob, and they all came to the king.

Saul said, "Listen now, son of Ahitub."

"Yes, my lord," he answered.

Saul said to him, "Why have you conspired against me, you and the son of Jesse, giving him bread and a sword and inquiring of God for him, so that he has rebelled against me and lies in wait for me, as he does today?"

Ahimelech answered the king, "Who of all your servants is as loyal as David, the king's son-in-law, captain of your bodyguard and highly respected in your household? Was that day the first time I inquired of God for him? Of course not! Let not the king accuse your servant or any of his father's family, for your servant knows nothing at all about this whole affair."

But the king said, "You will surely die, Ahimelech, you and your father's whole family."

Then the king ordered the guards at his side: "Turn and kill the priests of the LORD, because they too have sided with David. They knew he was fleeing, yet they did not tell me."

But the king's officials were not willing to raise a hand to strike the priests of the LORD.

The king then ordered Doeg, "You turn and strike down the priests." So Doeg the Edomite turned and struck them down. That day he killed eighty-five men who wore the linen ephod. He also put to the sword Nob, the town of the priests, with its men and women, its children and infants, and its cattle, donkeys and sheep.

But Abiathar, a son of Ahimelech son of Ahitub, escaped and fled to join David. He told David that Saul had killed the priests of the LORD. Then David said to Abiathar: "That day, when Doeg the Edomite was there, I knew he would be sure to tell Saul. I am responsible for the death of your father's whole family. Stay with me; don't be afraid; the man who is seeking your life is seeking mine also. You will be safe with me." (1 Samuel 22:6-23)

What a tragic story! David immediately recognized that part of the responsibility for this horrible slaughter was his. No, he didn't wield the sword that killed these priests and their families. But David had not recognized that if Saul were so emotionally unstable that he was irrationally trying to take the life of the only bright light in Israel militarily, then he also might have some other enemies that he was trying to get rid of as well. Saul was obsessed with jealousy and paranoia. He not only was bent on killing young David, but he also was looking at the priests as a challenge to his power as well. The priests were a strong force in Israel as they should have been. The priests represented the people to God. The priests taught God's laws and commandments to the people. The priests were generally respected and honored. And Saul was jealous of their influence. Instead of allying himself with the priests so that God's blessing and power could be with him on the throne, Saul opposed the priests and had even cut himself off from Samuel, the leader of the priests. David, too late, realized that he had given Saul an opportunity to avenge himself on those innocent priests. David, too late, realized the opportunism of this wicked Edomite named Doeg.

This event alone could have crushed most young people. But instead of being crushed, David grew from it. While recognizing his own lack of wisdom, he also realized that he had not made the decision to kill those priests and their families. That was Saul's decision. And David chose to learn an invaluable lesson concerning those who would use opportunistic situations to their own wicked ends as Doeg had.

Psalm 52 was written just after this tragic event occurred. Psalm 52 was David's response to Doeg and his despicable actions. This Psalm divides itself into three major sections. First, David exposes the wicked character of Doeg in the first four verses. Then David speaks of the brevity of Doeg's apparent success, that God will certainly thwart his ill-conceived plan, in the middle three verses. And finally, David renews his own faith and trust in the Lord in the last two verses of the Psalm.

Why do you boast of evil, you mighty man? Why do you boast all day long, you who are a disgrace in the eyes of God? Your tongue plots destruction; it is like a sharpened razor, you who practice deceit. You love evil rather than good, falsehood rather than speaking the truth. You love every harmful word, O you deceitful tongue!

Surely God will bring you down to everlasting ruin: He will snatch you up and tear you from your tent; he will uproot you from the land of the living. The righteous will see and fear; they will laugh at him, saying, "Here now is the man who did not make God his stronghold but trusted in his great wealth and grew strong by destroying others!"

But I am like an olive tree flourishing in the house of God; I trust in God's unfailing love forever and ever. I will praise you forever for what you have done; in your name I will hope, for your name is good. I will praise you in the presence of your saints. (Psalm 52:1-9)

David begins this Psalm with a question that is filled with satire and irony. *Why do you boast of evil, you mighty man?* Oh, you are just a courageous warrior, Doeg. After all, you killed all of those priests who didn't even have one weapon among them. Then you slaughtered their families. And then you bragged about your heroic conquests. You are such a mighty man. But while Doeg might have tried to convince himself that he was being loyal to Saul, in reality, he was a disgrace in the eyes of God. *Why do you boast all day long, you who are a disgrace in the eyes of God? (Psalm 52:1)*

David then goes on to expose Doeg's actions as being deceitful. *Your tongue plots destruction; it is like a sharpened razor, you who practice deceit. (Psalm 52:2)* The nuances of difference between David's commentary in this Psalm and the historical accounts from Samuel are interesting to note. When David first came to Ahimelech, the priest was very suspicious and reticent to offer any help. But it was David who convinced the priest of his need and the needs of the men who were with him. But when Doeg gives his testimony as an eyewitness to Saul, he makes it seem like Ahimelech was part of a conspiracy against the king. Ahimelech inquired of God for David and then he offered to him food and a weapon. It is clear that Doeg misrepresents the whole situation. He does so probably because he knew that he was telling Saul what the king wanted to hear. But he also probably did so because he knew it was to his own political advantage. Saul had just offered great rewards to anyone who would step forward with help. Doeg had just been Saul's chief shepherd up to this point. He saw this situation as a golden opportunity for advancement perhaps even to a prominent place in the palace.

But David moved beyond the inhumanity of the actions to the evilness in Doeg's heart. *You love evil rather than good, falsehood rather than speaking the truth. You love every harmful word, O you deceitful tongue. (Psalm 52:3,4)* David correctly identified the wickedness that festered within Doeg's depraved heart. He was just a cruel and evil man. Anyone who would be a party to killing eighty-five innocent families had to just revel in wickedness. This was such a despicable act that none of the other loyal members of Saul's household would even touch it. They all refused even the king's command because it was so immoral. But not Doeg. He jumped at the chance for advancement, even though it meant the loss of innocent lives.

Doeg's plan was doomed to fail. God would certainly not allow this wicked plot of his to succeed. So David, in faith, speaks of the brief nature of his apparent success. *Surely God will bring you down to everlasting ruin; he will snatch you up and tear you from your tent; he will uproot you from the land of the living. (Psalm 52:5)*

There is an increasing intensity in the verbs that David used to describe Doeg's fate. *Bring you down - snatch you up - tear you from your tent - uproot you.* Just as Doeg had been the weapon in Saul's hand to bring about the annihilation of innocent people who were serving the Lord, so he would suffer the same fate. What he had sown, he would also reap. God would never let this travesty of justice go unpunished. Doeg would spend the rest of his life looking over his shoulder, waiting for God's hand of justice and judgment to fall upon him.

And when Doeg became the recipient of God's justice, he would become an object lesson for everyone in the whole nation. *The righteous will see and fear; they will laugh at him, saying, "Here now is the man who did not make God his stronghold but trusted in his great wealth and grew strong by destroying others." (Psalm 52:7)*
Again, the progression is most interesting and instructive.

*they will **see** - they will observe what God is doing and recognize that it is the just recompense for his wicked actions.

*they will **fear** - they will acknowledge that God is powerful and mighty and able to execute his justice even upon the most powerful leaders on this earth

*they will **laugh** - they will ridicule and make fun of Doeg. Here was a man who wanted desperately to climb the political ladder. He wanted power, acceptance, fame and adulation.   But in the end, he would just receive ridicule, a most humbling experience.

David concluded this Psalm with a reaffirmation of his own trust and faith in the Lord. *But I am like an olive tree flourishing in the house of God; I trust in God's unfailing love forever and ever. I will praise you forever for what you have done; in your name I will hope, for your name is good. I will praise you in the presence of your saints. (Psalm 52:8,9)*

The olive tree symbolizes many things to the Jewish mind and all of them are good.

*It pictures prosperity for the olive tree produces the best yield for the amount of work of any plant in Israel.

*It pictures beauty for the rugged appearance of the olive tree is a beautiful sight to the Jewish eye. It was the custom for Jewish women to adorn themselves with olive branches at festivals to make them look more attractive.

*It pictures strength for the olive tree is able to stand firm and tall even amidst the most violent storms. It is interesting that some centuries later when the Greeks would initiate the Olympic Games that olive wreaths would be chosen to honor those who were victorious in the contests.

*It pictures endurance for the olive tree is a plant that can live a long, long life. Even to this day, when one visits the Garden of Gethsemane where Jesus sweat great drops of blood on the night of his betrayal, one can see ancient olive trees that possibly witnessed those events. *Gethsemane* means the olive press. It was the place where olives were harvested and processed. And there remain there to this day trees that have stood for centuries upon centuries.

*It pictures holiness for the olive provided oil for the lamps in the temple of God itself.

If a poll were to be taken in Israel when David wrote this Psalm, Doeg might well have been voted more likely to succeed than David. After all, Doeg was now in Saul's inner circle. Doeg was on his way to the top. David was the fugitive. David was a man with little hope for a future. But David was a man of integrity. He trusted in the righteous character of God. So in faith, he spoke of Doeg's demise and his own success in God's timing.

I wish I could produce an historic account of what happened to Doeg the Edomite. We know nothing more about him other than what we have discussed in this chapter. He is not referred to in the Bible again after the account in 1 Samuel. But perhaps that fact says volumes. For in the continuing account of Saul, Doeg is not mentioned among his advisers or counselors or cabinet. It is likely that Doeg was quickly seen for the evil opportunist that he was and discarded, even by King Saul. One day, we will know the end of Doeg's story in glory.

But we do know that David continued to grow and learn lessons that would enable him to become a most successful leader. And one lesson that David learned very clearly from this event in his life was to **never trust a person who appeared to be an opportunist.** For when David finally would become king of Israel, there would be many who would try to take advantage of his position and power. But David would remain a person of integrity and establish a throne based upon honesty and righteousness.

Saul, on the other hand, would end up taking his own life in a battle with the Philistines. The Bible records that Saul was severely wounded. He chose to take his own life by falling on his sword rather than be taken alive into the Philistine camp.

But do you remember the story about the Amalekite who witnessed Saul's death? This man saw an immediate opportunity for advancement in the next regime. So this Amalekite grabbed Saul's crown and armband and brought them to David, using them as evidence that he had killed Saul. He was an opportunist. He expected David to welcome the news and reward him handsomely. But do you remember what David said and did? The record in the first chapter of 2 Samuel speaks volumes about the lessons that David had learned from Doeg.

David asked him, "Why were you not afraid to lift your hand to destroy the Lord's anointed?" Then David called one of his men and said, "Go, strike him down." So he struck him down, and he died. For David had said to him, "Your blood be on your own head. Your own mouth testified against you when you said, 'I killed the Lord's anointed.'" (2 Samuel 1:14,15)

When David saw that opportunistic Amalekite coming with Saul's crown in his hand, could it be that he saw Doeg the Edomite? David had learned the lesson of dealing with those who would be opportunistic, and that lesson would help his kingdom to be built upon a strong foundation of integrity and trust.

We live in a world where opportunism so often appears to be rewarded. But we must never forget to see deceit, hypocrisy and dishonesty through the eyes of God. We must always remember that what appears to work in the short run cannot stand up to what God has decreed to be successful in the long run.

God's character remains the same. He is righteous and just; he is a God of absolute integrity and honesty; and he is a God who rewards those who diligently seek Him. God is still looking for people after His own heart.

PRAISE FROM A CAVE
Chapter 4

A derrick is an apparatus that hoists or moves heavy weights. But few construction engineers today remember that the derricks they use to make their jobs so much easier are named after a man named Godfrey Derrick who lived in the 17th century. Godfrey was London's hangman. It was his job to execute prisoners who had been condemned to capital punishment. And he performed his job with a professional efficiency unknown before by others in his office.

You see, before Godfrey was commissioned hangman, the gallows at Tyburn (today the northeast corner of Hyde Park) was a rather simple tripod. Three long legs were arranged so that a rope could be suspended where their tops joined. It was Godfrey Derrick who redesigned the gallows. He fixed a long beam horizontally from the top of a platform so that the noose could be moved out to the end of the beam. Now prisoners could be hanged without the inconvenience of having the legs of the gallows getting in the way and with better visibility for the crowds that inevitably gathered in the park to witness the executions. No wonder the people of London soon were calling the Tyburn gallows *the derrick* in honor of its inventor.

But it was on those gallows that Godfrey Derrick had designed that a great irony of justice was to occur. For it had only been a few months before Derrick had become London's hangman that he had been in a rather treacherous position himself. Godfrey had been arrested in the French city of Calais on the charge of rape. He had been tried and convicted in court and sentenced to be hanged. Desperate to save his own life, Derrick had contacted the British authorities to intercede on his behalf. Robert, the Earl of Essex, had taken pity upon him. Robert had traveled to Calais and used his influence to have Derrick's sentence commuted. Godfrey Derrick was released from prison and sent back to England where he became London's hangman. But Derrick had just been at his new position for a little more than a year when he was given what must have been his most difficult assignment. Robert, the Earl of Essex, had fallen from grace and was condemned to be hanged by the king. Here was the man who had saved his neck, but now Godfrey Derrick was asked to execute him. If he was disturbed by the task, he hid it well. For history records that, with his usual brisk efficiency, Godfrey Derrick strung up the Earl of Essex and took his life.

What an irony! One man who saves another from the hangman's noose only to be executed by the very person he saved. What an injustice! One man who risks a great deal to save another who had been convicted of a crime only to be executed as an innocent man. But this was not the first time that such an irony of injustice occurred.

In studying the early life of David, the many injustices that he suffered are most disturbing. Here was a young man who was as loyal a subject to King Saul as anyone could have been. Here was a young man who had risked his life for his country by going out alone to duel the giant Goliath. Here was a young man who had sacrificed for the wellbeing of the king, being away from home for long periods of time so that he could be the court musician to soothe Saul's troubled spirit. Any light that Israel had as a nation at this time was due to David. Without David's confrontation with Goliath, the Israelites would have been under the complete domination of the Philistines. Saul wouldn't have even been a functioning king in practical reality. He would have just been a puppet under Philistine control. The fact that Saul had any autonomy at all and that Israel as a nation had any hope for the future was due to David's courage and spirit. David had saved Saul's life and kingship. But, amazingly, despite all that David had done for Saul, the King of Israel was obsessed with this young man's destruction.

Happily, David learned some major lessons during his long exile from the king's palace and from his home. For Saul's obsession to kill David became so severe that David had to run for his life. He had to flee to the caves of Adullam and live the life of a fugitive and vagabond. His was certainly a life of inconvenience at best and terrified apprehension at worst. There were periods of time when Saul just left him alone because there were more pressing matters for his consideration. But there were also times when Saul led his armies out to search for David with orders to kill him on sight. Throughout this decade of trial in his life, however, David grew in his character, in his military savvy and in his walk with the Lord.

Psalm 57 was written from one of those caves where David was hiding from Saul. This psalm is representative of the several psalms that David wrote under those similar conditions for it reveals the reality of both his dangerous situation as well as his trust in the Lord.

Psalm 57 falls naturally into three sections. First, there is a cry for help as David calls upon the Lord to save him in his time of need. Then David speaks of a crisis that was harmful to him. And finally, there is a confession of hope in the Lord as David renews his trust in God even in the midst of his difficulties.

David is a godly model for facing dangerous situations. Now none of us probably has a powerful person stalking us with a large army in an attempt to take our lives. Happily, there are laws against stalking today. But we all face dangerous situations in life. Our dangerous situation might be a health related issue, or it might be a fellow student at school who is threatening us, or it might be a tenuous work environment, or it might even be an explosive family powder-keg. Most of us are tempted to go to one of two extremes in handling dangerous situations. We either become overwhelmed by the danger and paralyzed by fear so that we can't think or react in a constructive manner or we go into denial by just pretending that the dangerous situation doesn't exist and just wait for the inevitable to occur. But Psalm 57 shows us how David avoided those two extremes. David had the courage to face threatening situations realistically. He was willing to admit the dangers and even talk about them. But he never lost perspective. He didn't allow his fearful circumstances to become bigger than God.

This Psalm begins with David's cry for help.

Have mercy on me, O God, have mercy on me, for in you my soul takes refuge. I will take refuge in the shadow of your wings until the disaster has passed. I cry out to God Most High, to God, who fulfills his purpose for me. He sends from heaven and saves me, rebuking those who hotly pursue me; God sends his love and his faithfulness. (Psalm 57:1-3)

David is in trouble here and he knows it. He cries out to God for help. He pleads for God's mercy. He recognizes his need for outside help to be delivered from his predicament.

But even in the midst of his plea for help, David continues to maintain his perspective on the situation. Yes, Saul was a powerful man. It was true that he had threatening resources at his disposal. And David knew that Saul had committed himself to his destruction. But Saul and his power were nothing compared to God. David uses the name *God Most High* in addressing God. This was the term used in the Bible to recognize God as the only true and living God, above all other humanly made gods or earthly powers. And then David also speaks of a God *who fulfills his purpose for me.* David knew that God had a plan for his life. David had received the anointing oil from Samuel's flask. David had been told of God's purpose in giving to him the throne of Israel. Yes, it certainly appeared that the situation had gotten out of God's control. But David trusted in a God who was all-knowing and had the power to execute his will. So even in the midst of this physical danger, sitting in a barren cave with adversaries stalking his very life, David called out to God for mercy and help.

But let's move on now to consider **the crisis that was harmful to David's wellbeing.**

I am in the midst of lions; I lie among ravenous beasts -- men whose teeth are spears and arrows, whose tongues are sharp swords. Be exalted, O God, above the heavens; let your glory be over all the earth. They spread a net for my feet -- I was bowed down in distress. They dug a pit in my path -- but they have fallen into it themselves. (Psalm 57:4-6)

Now David certainly had reason to fear wild beasts for they often made their homes in these very caves where David was hiding. David knew that he could easily walk into one of the caves that dot the rugged hillside of the Negev and find a lion or pack of wild dogs living inside.

But we know that David was using the term *lion* in a figurative sense in speaking of King Saul and his men in this passage because he goes on to speak of men who were intent on doing him harm.

And it is most interesting that David picks out two specific areas of concern here. First, there was certainly the most obvious physical danger that Saul had placed upon him. So David speaks of men whose teeth are spears and arrows. Saul and his followers were not content to stop until a spear or arrow had pierced David's heart. They were intent upon his complete destruction.

But then David moves to another area of concern, one which we might be tempted to overlook, but was a real potential problem for him. He goes on to say *men whose tongues are sharp swords.* David was not only concerned with Saul's spear, but he was also aware of Saul's tongue. David knew that the king was spreading lies and untrue stories about him all the time that he was hunting him, deceitful rumors that could mar and ruin David's reputation. David realized that, as the next anointed king, his name and reputation would be most important to him. So he was concerned about the harmful damage that was being done to his reputation as he was hiding out in a cave, as he was unable to defend himself in any way. Even David's running as a fugitive might lead some people to assume his guilt. And David knew that Saul would use every possible advantage at his disposal. David knew the destructive power of the gossip that Saul was spreading about him and it concerned him. It seemed to concern him as much as the physical danger of Saul's swords, spears and arrows.

It is true that there is great power in words. Someone has anonymously written a brief poem entitled *Small Beginnings:*

A snowflake is so very small we scarcely think of it at all,

And yet enough of them will make a barrier that we cannot break.

A drop of water is so slight that as it falls it fades from sight,

And yet enough of them will be a torrent or a raging sea.

A word is but a breath of air, tis heard or spoken without care.

Yet words in fierce profusion hurled upset the history of the world.

David's confidence in this real danger was that God could and would overrule Saul's lies by revealing his true character so that David's reputation would not be completely damaged. And that is exactly what happened. Instead of people believing Saul's lies and thinking poorly about David, they began to see Saul's instability of character and began to think that David must be a very special and gifted man if Saul were so intent upon his destruction. As time progressed, Saul's lies and lack of discretion in spreading untrue gossip actually turned on him and damaged his reputation.

Lessons can be learned not only from the positive example of David, but also from the negative example of Saul. For when we fail to control our tongues, we do great damage to ourselves and our reputations. If we gain a reputation for spreading gossip or untrue stories, then people eventually will not take anything we say credibly or respect us personally. Oh, they might want to hear the latest newsy morsel from our lips, but they really won't respect us personally.

When our family traveled for just over a month in England some years ago now, we enjoyed visiting many old churches. Every old church that we saw in England has a graveyard beside it where parishioners down through the centuries have been laid to rest. There was one drab, gray slate tombstone that I read which said volumes about how the people regarded the deceased whose body was buried there. It simply read: *Beneath this stone, a lump of clay, lies Arabella Young, who, on the 24th of May, began to hold her tongue.*

One of the poorest reputations that a person can have in life is that of a gossip, one who spreads stories and lies about others. That was the reputation that Saul gained before he died, and it cost him the respect and honor of the kingship. But David did not retaliate. He really wasn't in a position to do so even if he had so desired. But David chose to commit the matter to the Lord.

Now, as was noted earlier in this chapter, it is critically important that we see the fact that David admitted and faced the harmful crisis that confronted him. David had to physically run for his life and hide in a cave. His only other alternative was to raise up a mutinous rebellion against Saul and try to overthrow the throne. David knew that this would be a wrong response and would set a horrible precedent of instability for the nation. But David did not succumb to the temptation of running emotionally as well. He did not deny his dangerous situation. He did not lie to himself. He rather faced his dangers. This is what makes David such an example of courage. For courageous people are not those who face no dangers, nor are they people who have no fear in

54

danger. David had real dangers and he felt real fear in the midst of those dangers. But courageous people are those who are willing to face their fears and ask for help from a source that can provide the help. There is tremendous freedom experienced when dangers are faced and help is secured.

A couple who is having difficulties in a marriage is courageous when they admit those problems that they are having and seek out the help of a good counselor who can guide them to better communication. This becomes a freeing experience in a relationship.

A student who is being bullied by someone at school is courageous when he admits the problem that he is having and seeks out help in facing the bully. What a freeing experience it is when a young person faces that bully with an older friend and becomes released from that awful grip.

A person who is experiencing some serious health symptoms is courageous when she makes an appointment with the doctor and has some tests run. As long as there is denial, fear and anxiety rule. But when the symptoms are faced there is the freeing experience of knowing exactly what the health issue is so some steps can be taken towards a cure.

Whenever fears are denied, they just become bigger and more complicated. When fears are faced and dealt with, there is freedom and relief. David knew this principle.

But finally, we see **David's confession of hope.**

My heart is steadfast, O God, my heart is steadfast; I will sing and make music. Awake, my soul! Awake, harp and lyre! I will awaken the dawn. I will praise you, O Lord, among the nations; I will sing of you among the peoples.

For great is your love, reaching to the heavens; your faithfulness reaches to the skies. Be exalted, O God, above the heavens; let your glory be over all the earth. (Psalm 57:7-11)

Music in the midst of madness. Praise in the midst of persecution. Worship instead of worry. Those were David's choices. He refused to allow the threats of Saul to rob him of his song in life.

How did David reach this position where he could sing from the cave where he was hiding? He was humble enough to cry out to God for help; he was honest enough to admit the crisis that was harmful to him; and he had faith to confess his hope in the Lord in the midst of his struggles.

And what is most interesting to note was the fact that David's joy and confidence was not expressed only after Saul had finally been killed and he had become recognized as the king of Israel. No, this joy came from David as he was sitting alone in a barren cave. David found joy in the midst of the dangerous situation. Anyone can have joy when the danger is passed. But only God can give joy in the midst of the trial. But we can only find that joy as we find it in God himself.

One of the most traumatic events that any country endures is the assassination of its leader. Certainly the most trying moments in our country's history have been the times when our presidents have been shot while in office. Many still remember where they were when President Kennedy was assassinated and when President Reagan was shot. William McKinley was the 25th president of the United States. During his first term, our country made great advances both at home and abroad. We won the Spanish-American war further entrenching our position as a world power. And business and industry were booming at the turn of the twentieth century. But it was just six months into his second term of office that McKinley became our third president to be assassinated.

When President Reagan was shot, he was rushed to a hospital, x-rays were taken to determine the exact location of the bullet, and an operation was performed so that the bullet could be removed. His life was spared. President William McKinley was at the 1901 Pan American Exposition in Buffalo, New York, giving a speech when he was shot. He was rushed into a tent where the best medical personnel available were called to assist him. They operated, trying to locate and remove the bullet, but they could not find the exact location of the bullet at first. By the time the extensive exploratory operation was completed, McKinley's body was so severely weakened by the procedure that eight days later, he died in Buffalo.

The irony of President McKinley's death was that a new invention that was being introduced to the world for the very first time at that Pan American Exposition was sitting one tent over from where he was being worked on by the medical personnel. This new invention was called an x-ray machine. We know today that it could have saved President McKinley's life if it would have only been used. But in the chaos and panic of the moment, nobody even thought of that x-ray machine. It was considered to be only an experimental exhibit. That day, our country lost its premiere leader.

How many people, in the chaos and panic of their dangerous dilemma, forget that there is a loving, all-knowing and all-powerful God who is just a prayer away, who is more than willing to step in, giving his help and strength in our time of need? David remembered. This allowed him to have a song of joy in the midst of imminent

danger.   This allowed David to express praise even from a
cave.

History is filled with examples of God's sovereignty, guiding human affairs through small, seemingly insignificant events. One such time occurred in June of 1776, during our Revolutionary War. New York's Colonial Governor, William Tryon, was a loyal supporter of the third King George. From a British gunboat in New York's harbor, he was doing his best to sabotage the small, revolutionary army through personal relationships that he had made. Tryon had devised an ingenious plan to ambush the Continental Army from behind their lines with their own weapons. The final blow would be to capture General George Washington and hand him over to the British, dead or alive.

The plan certainly had good potential to work. It was carefully laid out even to the smallest detail. But as the key leaders were going over their final details in the Sergeant Arm's Tavern, a waiter overheard enough to understand what being plotted. He tipped off some loyal revolutionaries that he knew. Within a day, forty key ringleaders who had been involved in the treacherous plot had been identified and rounded up. Among them was David Matthews who was then the mayor of New York City and Thomas Hickey who was George Washington's personal bodyguard.

During Hickey's interrogation, it was Washington's own trusted bodyguard who revealed the most amazing plot of all. He confessed to having poisoned some peas that were to be a part of General Washington's meal one day. For some mysterious reason, the man who loved this vegetable did not have a taste for them on that specific day so the peas were thrown out as food for the chickens with some other scraps. Other household servants remembered several chickens that had suddenly died in the night but had not thought to connect their deaths to the poisoned peas. The court found Thomas Hickey guilty of mutiny, sedition and treachery and he was hanged on June 28, 1776.

It must be a very unsettling feeling to find out that a trusted friend who was given the responsibility of being a personal bodyguard has turned to the other side and betrayed the one who has placed such confidence in him. But these things happen at times in life. And one who is destined to be a leader, like George Washington, must develop the ability to cope with such disappointments and also have the faith to trust in a God who is able to overrule even the best laid human plans.

We come now to an event in David's life where he learned such a lesson. Most political systems work on a give and take assumption. Even a king who supposedly has absolute power must work with and through other people in order to accomplish anything. One leader will do a favor for another, and then expect a reciprocal favor in return. We have a saying: *if you scratch my back, I'll scratch yours*. Nowhere is this saying realized in a purer sense than in the political arena.

In the final analysis, this whole system of thinking and acting relies upon careful planning and plotting and a confidence in people to pay back the debts of favors that are owed if they expect to have more favors in due time. But a lifetime operating in such a system can bring great disillusionment. For every action is suspect for some ulterior motive. So whether the politics are in Washington, or in the business office, or in any other organization, they can become very suspect and actually undermine integrity and sincerity of good will.

There is a great deal of difference in loving our neighbor because it is the right thing to do and loving our neighbor so that we can get a favor from them in return. The difference isn't necessarily in the benevolent action that is performed, but it is certainly evident in the motive. That is the reason for Jesus giving the parable of the *Good Samaritan* in response to the question *who is my neighbor?* The priest and Levite who passed by the wounded man on that road from Jerusalem to Jericho didn't help the man in such great need because they didn't see much possibility for good in return.

These were men who did many good deeds in life. Certainly, society would respect them as being wonderful people. But their good deeds were directed toward those who had the ability to reciprocate. The Samaritan, on the other hand, acted in kindness, expecting nothing in return. So Christ's point was, if we really love our neighbors, we should give of ourselves to them, not expecting a return for our investment.

David learned this lesson all too painfully in a situation that developed in the small town of Keilah. Keilah was located near the border of Israeli and Philistine controlled territories. It's a most fascinating story.

When David was told, "Look, the Philistines are fighting against Keilah and are looting the threshing floors," he inquired of the LORD, saying, "Shall I go and attack these Philistines?"

The LORD answered him, "Go, attack the Philistines and save Keilah."

But David's men said to him, "Here in Judah we are afraid. How much more, then, if we go to Keilah against the Philistine forces!"

61

Once again David inquired of the LORD, and the LORD answered him, "Go down to Keilah, for I am going to give the Philistines into your hand." So David and his men went to Keilah, fought the Philistines and carried off their livestock. He inflicted heavy losses on the Philistines and saved the people of Keilah.   (Now Abiathar son of Ahimelech had brought the ephod down with him when he fled to David at Keilah.)

Saul was told that David had gone to Keilah, and he said, "God has handed him over to me, for David has imprisoned himself by entering a town with gates and bars."   And Saul called up all his forces for battle, to go down to Keilah to besiege David and his men.

When David learned that Saul was plotting against him, he said to Abiathar the priest, "Bring the ephod." David said, "O LORD, God of Israel, your servant has heard definitely that Saul plans to come to Keilah and destroy the town on account of me.   Will the citizens of Keilah surrender me to him? Will Saul come down, as your servant has heard? O LORD, God of Israel, tell your servant."

And the LORD said, "He will."

Again David asked, "Will the citizens of Keilah surrender me and my men to Saul?"

And the LORD said, "They will."

So David and his men, about six hundred in number, left Keilah and kept moving from place to place. When Saul was told that David had escaped from Keilah, he did not go there. David stayed in the desert strongholds and in the hills of the Desert of Ziph. Day after day Saul searched for him, but God did not give David into his hands.

While David was at Horesh in the Desert of Ziph, he learned that Saul had come out to take his life. And Saul's son Jonathan went to David at Horesh and helped him find strength in God. "Don't be afraid," he said. "My father Saul will not lay a hand on you. You will be king over Israel, and I will be second to you. Even my father Saul knows this." The two of them made a covenant before the LORD. Then Jonathan went home, but David remained at Horesh.

The Ziphites went up to Saul at Gibeah and said, "Is not David hiding among us in the strongholds at Horesh, on the hill of Hakilah, south of Jeshimon? Now, O king, come down whenever it pleases you to do so, and we will be responsible for handing him over to the king."

Saul replied, "The LORD bless you for your concern for me. Go and make further preparation. Find out where David usually goes and who has seen him there. They tell me he is very crafty. Find out about all the hiding places he uses and come back to me with definite information. Then I will go with you; if he is in the area, I will track him down among all the clans of Judah."

So they set out and went to Ziph ahead of Saul. Now David and his men were in the Desert of Maon, in the Arabah south of Jeshimon. Saul and his men began the search, and when David was told about it, he went down to the rock and stayed in the Desert of Maon. When Saul heard this, he went into the Desert of Maon in pursuit of David.

Saul was going along one side of the mountain, and David and his men were on the other side, hurrying to get away from Saul. As Saul and his forces were closing in on David and his men to capture them, a messenger came to Saul, saying, "Come quickly! The Philistines are raiding the land." Then Saul broke off his pursuit of David and went to meet the Philistines. That is why they call this place Sela Hammahlekoth. And David went up from there and lived in the strongholds of En Gedi. (1 Samuel 23:1-29)

The poor citizens of Keilah were in a situation that could have proved to be economically disastrous for them. They had just finished harvesting their crops and now they were threshing the grain. But the Philistines had now attacked the city. The Keilahites were powerless to oppose the stronger Philistine army. So they were in danger of losing all of the fruit of their labors. The Philistines were planning to take away all of their harvest leaving them in dire economic straits. How would you like to lose a year's wages? That was what was happening to the citizens of Keilah.

Now this sad situation reveals the weakness and ineptitude of Saul's leadership at this time. It was King Saul's job to defend the citizens of Israel against Philistine oppression. But he was so wrapped up in his own emotional problems and his obsession with finding and killing David that his constituency was suffering greatly.

But now David comes along. David takes his comparatively few fighting men and courageously attacks the Philistines, saving the city of Keilah from physical and economic disaster. What a debt these citizens owed to David! He had saved their harvest and had undoubtedly saved many of their lives as well. And David well might have assumed that he would finally have a decent place to live with his men. No longer would their families have to run from cave to cave. Now they would have houses within the protection of a city wall in which to live. The citizens of Keilah would also have a police force to protect their town. It seemed like a win-win situation.

But when King Saul heard that David had settled in the city of Keilah and when he gathered together his forces to try to take him, the true colors of the Keilahite loyalty came out, didn't it? After all David had done for them, they were still going to hand him over to Saul. So David had to flee again for his life.

Back to the Negev region; back to the desert area; back to the caves again. And no sooner had David settled in this barren wilderness than he received another blow. He learned that the nomadic Ziphites had also turned on him betraying his location to Saul. So Saul was again on his trail. This time, only a miraculous intervention by God would save David from Saul's hand.

The irony of these situations is found in the fact that both the citizens of Keilah and the Ziphites were trying to play the political game and both lost. They both thought if they turned in David to Saul they would gain something in return. But King Saul wasn't in a position to do any favors for them. And both the citizens of Keilah and the Ziphites lost a very valuable ally and defender in David.

But the one person who stood by David loyally was Jonathan. To all outward appearances, Jonathan had everything to lose and nothing to gain in his friendship with David. Jonathan was Saul's son. Under normal circumstances, Jonathan would have been next in line for the throne of Israel. Having been anointed by the prophet Samuel, David could have appeared to be a rival to the throne that Jonathan could well have assumed to be his possession.

But Jonathan saw the injustice that David was suffering and he stood by David because Jonathan was a man of integrity. He knew it was the right thing to do. Jonathan was sincere in his motives expecting nothing in return for his friendship with David. And it is Jonathan who ends up with the future blessings. For Jonathan's family was honored by David and even ended up dining at the palace when he finally became king.

David wrote Psalm 54 in response to this scene in 1 Samuel 23. It was a Psalm written out of a situation that potentially could have been so disillusioning and disheartening for this young leader. But this Psalm reveals some invaluable lessons that David learned from this experience.

Save me, O God, by your name; vindicate me by your might. Hear my prayer, O God; listen to the words of my mouth. Strangers are attacking me; ruthless men seek my life -- men without regard for God.

Surely God is my help; the Lord is the one who sustains me. Let evil recoil on those who slander me; in your faithfulness destroy them.

I will sacrifice a freewill offering to you; I will praise your name, O LORD, for it is good. For he has delivered me from all my troubles, and my eyes have looked in triumph on my foes. (Psalm 54:1-7)

David's prayer to God is summarized in the first verse. It was really a **two-fold prayer**: *Save me and vindicate me.* David was concerned for his physical safety for this situation where Saul had him cornered on the other side of the mountain was just too close for comfort. But David was also concerned for his reputation. The word *vindicate* is a judicial term. Saul had judged him and pronounced him to be guilty without any evidence or a trial. David called upon God to vindicate him. He called upon God to demonstrate his innocence.

David continued on to develop these two concerns in the next verses. Verse three elaborates on his prayer for God to save him. *Strangers are attacking me: ruthless men seek my life - men without regard for God.* Godless men who were only trying to play political games to

66

advance their own careers were using David as a pawn in their chess match. They felt that David's death would enhance their careers. David knew the danger that such men posed, and he prayed to God for deliverance from them.

Then David goes on to develop his concern for vindication in verse five. *Let evil recoil on those who slander me; in your faithfulness destroy them.* Saul's colleagues might slander his good name and the citizens of Keilah and the Ziphites might believe such lies and turn on David for their own selfish advantages, but God would remain faithful to him. David trusted in the absolute character of God never leaving nor forsaking His own and God's ability to execute his justice in His time.

These were very real dangers for David and he was concerned for them. But even in the midst of his prayer for help, David continued to place his faith and trust in the Lord. *Surely God is my help; the Lord is the one who sustains me. (Psalm 54:4)*

David's reliance upon a sovereign God who was faithful and just to save and vindicate him helped to deliver him from perhaps the greatest of all the dangers that he faced, the danger of becoming disillusioned and bitter. For the physical dangers would pass in time, and he would be able to gain his reputation back again. But if David would have succumbed to the temptations of disillusionment and bitterness, he might have carried these burdens for the rest of his life.

How easy it would have been for David to become disillusioned with human nature. After all, these citizens of Keilah and the Ziphites had turned on him after all that he had done for them. He had saved their lives and their livelihoods. David could have easily become an untrusting, cynical person. How easy it would have been for David to develop a bitter spirit. These turncoats continued to live in their fine houses more prosperous now than they had been before, thanks to his defeat of the Philistines, and he and his family and followers were again inconvenienced in these dirty caves. Life is so unfair. The good guys suffer while the ones who play the political games prosper. The ones who try to do what is right suffer while the treacherous betrayers prosper. But to David's credit, he did not allow a seed of bitterness to take root in his heart. He rather learned lessons from these situations, lessons that would stand him in good stead for the rest of his life.

David concluded this Psalm with a song of thanksgiving. *I will sacrifice a free will offering to you.* The freewill offering was a spontaneous gift to the Lord to express thanksgiving. David presented this offering because he had faith that God was going to deliver him. The verb tenses found in the last verse are most interesting. *For He has delivered me from all my troubles, and my eyes have looked in triumph on my foes. (Psalm 54: 7)*

One could easily argue with David that he still remained in danger when he was originally writing these words. Saul was still bent on killing him. It was still unsafe for him to travel freely. He still could not return to his family's inheritance. But David was so overwhelmed by the faithfulness of the Lord that he could even speak of his deliverance in past tense as if it had already occurred.

As this Psalm is considered in its totality, an excellent model for the believer facing endangering situations with great faith is discovered.

*David began by **praying for God to save him** and vindicate him.

*He then **faced his dangerous situation**. He spoke of his fear for his life and his reputation. He didn't run from his fears but faced them head on, identifying them.

*But David quickly moved from focusing on his fears to **focusing his eyes on the Lord.** He expressed confidence in the strength and might of God to be his protector.

*And David concluded by **expressing thanksgiving** in advance for the deliverance that he knew by faith God was going to give to him. This is certainly a model of great faith, faith that is expressed and thanksgiving that is offered even before the dangerous situation is totally resolved.

Happily, we don't usually face the same type of stalking that David had to endure. If we do, we need only call the authorities and have a judge issue a restraining order. But each of us faces dangerous situations. A dangerous situation is any circumstance that has the potential to bring great harm or trouble into our lives. Perhaps our dangerous situation involves an interpersonal relationship. Or perhaps our dangerous situation involves a family problem. Or perhaps our dangerous situation is very personal involving some inner struggle that we are having with some temptation. Or perhaps our dangerous situation involves a large business risk that we are presently taking.

Perhaps we need to be involved in a dangerous situation. Perhaps we are living life too much in our comfort zone and we need to take some risks. We must always remember the fact that God led David into these dangerous situations so that David's faith could be strengthened and he could learn some very important lessons. We all need to realize that the Lord is always there to help us. We all need to face our fears as painful as they might be. We all need to Identify our fears so that we can address them.

As we put our faith in the Lord, whatever our dangerous situation may be, we find God to be greater. He is able to deliver us. And we need to be quick to thank God for his hand of deliverance. It is impossible for a thankful heart to be a bitter heart. God desires for us to be thankful in all things, even in the dangerous situations of life.

Corrie ten Boom often told an account of her suffering in a concentration camp during World War 2 that illustrates this principle that David learned. Corrie, along with her sister, Betsie, had just been moved to a new prison at Ravensbruck during the second week of October. Barracks 28 where they were placed was filthy and over-crowded. It had been designed for four hundred people, but over three times that many prisoners had been jammed into the barracks. The room was very poorly lit with just one bare light bulb. The women instinctively knew of the unsanitary conditions by the smell of filth, sweat and human waste that permeated the place. But among the worst of all the inconveniences were the fleas. Barracks 28 was infested with fleas. Corrie and Betsie found this out immediately as they began to feel the bites around their ankles and legs.

After they had been in their new home for just a little while, Betsie said to Corrie, *this gives us a chance to put our morning devotions into practice. Remember, this morning we read from 1 Thessalonians: "Comfort the frightened, help the weak, be patient with everyone. See that none of you repays evil for evil, but always seek to do good to one another and to all. . . Rejoice always, pray constantly, give thanks in all circumstances; for this is the will of God in Christ Jesus."*

Are you trying to say that we should give thanks for these circumstances, Betsie? Corrie asked in amazement.

That's exactly what I am saying, Betsie replied.

What is there to give thanks for?

Well, there's the fact that we got placed in these barracks together. And there's the fact that they didn't find our Bible and take it away for we can continue to have our devotional times. And there's the fact that there are so many people in this barracks so we will have more people to hear the word of God. And then there are the filthy conditions and the fleas.

Hold on, Corrie interrupted Betsie. *I can see thanking God for those other things. But how can we thank God for the filthy conditions and the fleas.*

But the Bible tells us to give thanks in all circumstances. This is a good opportunity to put this passage into practice in our lives, Betsie stood firm.

So Betsie and Corrie ten Boom prayed and thanked God for Barracks 28, even for the filthy conditions and the fleas. And then they continued their lives of hard work eleven hours every day as prisoners.

Every day, they had a devotional service in which they read the Bible and sang a song or two and prayed. In a short time, the service attracted so many of their fellow prisoners who wanted to hear the Word of God that they had to go to two services a day to accommodate everyone.

It was only some time later when Betsie was in the sick bay that she overheard some guards commenting about Barracks 28. The guards said that they did not want to go near that place because it was so filthy and infested with fleas. Betsie could hardly wait to share this new insight with her sister Corrie. Because of the fleas, these ladies had been spared the harassment that most of the other women in the prison camp had suffered, and they had been free to have two services of worship daily without any fear of being found out.

Betsie and Corrie ten Boom had been placed in a most distressing situation. They had trusted in a Sovereign God and even thanked God for his deliverance before they knew why or how he was going to do it. And God had honored their faith by giving to them more freedom than any of the other prisoners would know. Betsie didn't make it through the war. She went home to be with the Lord before the concentration camps were liberated. But Corrie ten Boom not only survived the war, she was also used by God to testify of his goodness and to be a model of forgiveness for millions of people in the decades following World War 2.

David had to learn the lesson that he couldn't trust in other people for his protection and well being, but he had to place his life into the hands of a Sovereign God if he were to know true security. So even in the midst of difficult situations, David chose to trust in the Lord. He even came to the place where he could thank God for his deliverance in advance because he trusted in a God who would not let him down.

HOW LONG, O LORD?
Chapter 6

Jim Pattridge had a dream. He wanted to learn a martial art. But every time he tried to enroll in a class, he was turned down. Now Jim had strong arms and some coordination. But it was his kicking that was his drawback. Jim just wasn't a good kicker. But Jim was persistent. He kept applying to class after class until he was turned down twelve times. Finally, Scott Keifer, the master instructor at an academy called U.S.A. Karate, told Jim that he could enroll in his class as long as he did so to assist his son, Brandon. So on his thirteenth try, Jim Pattridge became a formal karate student.

Jim was so enthusiastic that he was soon passing most of the other students, even though they were far younger than he. To make a long story shorter, after three years of study, Jim had learned more than three hundred different martial art techniques. Scott made him an assistant instructor. And then on June 23, 1990, Jim Pattridge, at age forty-two, received his black belt in three different martial art forms.

Jim never did learn to kick nor would he ever be able to. But through his patience and hard work, he learned to compensate in other ways. For you see, Jim Pattridge left Vietnam as a Marine in 1966 on a stretcher, with a purple heart pinned to his chest. Jim had stepped on an exploding mine. But today, because of his enthusiastic attitude, patience and hard work, Jim Pattridge is a black belt in Karate - even though he is deaf in one ear, legally blind, partially paralyzed on his entire left side, and has nothing below his waist. Both of Jim's legs were blown off by the land mine.

We live in a day when natural abilities are exalted. Many people excuse failures and limit their successes by complaining. If only I had a mind like Bill Gates, or the jumping abilities of LeBron James, or the musical talent of the Eagles. But the one virtue that we all possess is often completely overlooked. This virtue is patience. For no amount of natural abilities will ever overcome the lack of patience and character. But with patience, many natural disabilities can eventually be overcome and even mediocre abilities can become very proficient.

An admirer once asked the gifted pianist Ignace Paderewski, *is it true that you still practice every day? Yes,* answered the veteran musician, *I play that piano at least six hours every day. You must have a world of patience,* continued the fan. *I have no more patience than anyone else,* answered Paderewski. *I just use mine.* There is a great deal of truth in Padrewski's words. Everyone has the potential for patience. There is not one person who doesn't have a potential for patience. Now it's true that some people have temperaments that tend to be more easy-going. But all of us share in our potential for patience. Some people just develop and use their patience more than others.

God knew that David would need to have a great deal of patience if he were to become the influential king that God intended for him to be. So in addition to the many other lessons that God taught David in preparing him for the throne, he also added patience to the list.

We don't know exactly how long David was in exile from his home and family, running for his life from Saul, but by figuring out the chronology of David's life we can assume that it must have been around ten to twelve years. A decade is a long time for anybody to endure exile from his or her home and family. But it is especially long for a young man who has been anointed to be the next king, who is just chomping at the bit to get started on his career. But God knew that David would never be able to reach his fullest potential unless he became a patient person. So he allowed him to be in exile year after year until this lesson was learned.

Now we don't want to imply that this lesson of patience came easily for David. Patience never comes easily. The Bible tells us that tribulations develop patience in our lives. Nor do we want to imply that David never became frustrated in impatience. In fact, Psalm 13 reveals some of David's frustration and impatience. No one is naturally patient. We all have a tendency towards impatience. We all naturally rebel when we are forced to wait.

There was a locksmith who had a sign in his window that read *"keys made while you wait."* Business was slow, so he hired a consultant to evaluate his business. The consultant made an interesting observation. *Why don't you change your sign? People naturally are impatient. They don't like to wait.* So the locksmith changed his sign to read *"keys made while you watch."* He soon noticed that business had picked up.

David didn't like to wait. We can identify with this because most of us don't like to wait either. But God had to instill patience into David's character in order to make him the kind of person who would become a great king. So David had to change his perspective from just waiting to watching God develop him personally. Happily, David allowed God to develop more patience in his life so that he could become a great king.

Psalm 13 is divided into three sections of two verses each making up the total of six verses. In the first pair of verses, David reveals his problem. David was frustrated and impatient. In the second couplet, David prays to the Lord and asks for help. So here we find David's petition. And finally, the last two verses reveal David's choice to trust in the Lord and allow him to develop the patience needed in his life.

First, we see David's problem.

How long, O LORD? Will you forget me forever? How long will you hide your face from me? How long must I wrestle with my thoughts and every day have sorrow in my heart? How long will my enemy triumph over me? (Psalm 13:1,2)

David's problem was that he was becoming impatient. This caused a great deal of frustration in his life. He cries out *how long* to the Lord four times in just these two verses. *How long, how long, how long, how long*? Oh, he had probably been able to console himself during those first few weeks and months that the trial would quickly pass. But then as year piled upon year, and as Saul continued his rule of insanity, and as David appeared to be farther from the throne than ever, the natural tendency would be to become more and more impatient.

But it is interesting to note that David's impatience was not over what we might think. It was not the inconvenience of his living conditions in the cave that he mentions here. It must have been miserable for David to raise a family with the inconvenience of jumping from cave to cave. No stability. None of the modern conveniences that the other Israelites took for granted in their homes. Never a clean floor, no comfortable bed or equipped kitchen area. You would think that David would have become very impatient with such living conditions, wouldn't you? But he doesn't mention any of his living inconveniences as the source of his impatience. It is not even his separation from his other family members. It can be traumatic to be separated from relatives. And David's situation was so severe that he had to actually move his parents from their home in Bethlehem outside the country to Moab for their safety. So David's relatives were so far from him that he couldn't visit them for years. But David doesn't mention this either as the source of his impatience. Rather, it was his feeling of God's absence that bothered him so much. It seemed like God had forgotten all about him wandering out there in the Negev region. It seemed like God was hiding his presence and fellowship from him. It seemed like God had taken all the joy from his heart. Where was God? It just didn't seem like David could go on any longer feeling like God had deserted him.

The same feelings that David had are usually at the root of the impatience that we often feel as well. When we become impatient in life, we usually wonder why God isn't moving faster than he is. We wonder if God has deserted us or forgotten all about us. We wonder why God doesn't appear to be working in our lives. It is amazing how almost any trial can be endured as long as we sense God's hands at work, developing and building character in us. But when we don't sense his presence, when we feel like he has deserted us, when we feel all alone, we have a tendency to become impatient with our circumstances.

In the midst of his feelings of impatience, David cries out in prayer to God.

Look on me and answer, O LORD my God. Give light to my eyes, or I will sleep in death; my enemy will say, "I have overcome him," and my foes will rejoice when I fall. (Psalm 13:3,4)

David's prayer is three fold:

*Look on me - notice me. Here I am all alone out here in the wilderness. Don't forget about me out here in the deserted Negev region. Look on me.
*Answer me - pay attention to my cries. Show concern for my plight. Show compassion for me in my helpless condition.
*Give light to my eyes - help me to see the purpose in all of this. Show me the path to safety. Help me to see the meaning in what is happening to me.

David felt so alone and deserted. It was as if he had become lost out there in some forgotten cave in the Negev region. It was as if God were so busy with the rest of the world that he had forgotten all about little David in this remote region. David felt like a little child on an observation deck at the airport frantically waving his arms as the plane carrying his mother is soaring off into the sky. Look at me, notice me down here. But in his heart he realizes that he is just a spot amongst many spots and that his mother probably can't even see him.

Many times we feel like David in life. When the stresses of life begin to overwhelm us like waves on a troubled sea, we wonder if God really sees us and notices our plight. After all, we feel so insignificant in the overall life of this planet. We are not famous people. We are not world decision makers. We are not the highly visible. Does God really notice us sitting in the corner of our little caves? Does God really see us; does he really hear and answer our prayers; will he really shine the light of his truth and wisdom upon our path so that we can know what direction to take in life? It is during times like these that we can so easily become impatient. When is God going to work? When is he finally going to act? When is God going to notice us?

We can all identify with David's feelings as he was writing this Psalm because we have all been there. How we respond when we feel so rejected and impatient is critical to our growth and success in life. The manner of David's response tells volumes about his character and spiritual maturity. You see, David realized that his feelings didn't always reflect reality. He realized that God hadn't disappeared just because he couldn't feel His presence. He realized that God's ears weren't deafened to his cries just because he didn't feel like he was getting through. David realized the very significant truth that God's purposes were being fulfilled in his life even when he didn't feel like it was happening. So David made a choice, a choice to trust in the Lord even when he was feeling impatient with God.

But I trust in your unfailing love; my heart rejoices in your salvation. I will sing to the LORD, for he has been good to me. (Psalm 13:5,6)

*In the midst of doubt, David chose to trust.

*In the midst of feelings of abandonment, David affirmed God's unfailing love.

*In the midst of feelings of sorrow, David chose to rejoice.

*In the presence of his enemies, David focused on God's salvation and deliverance.

*In the midst of his discouragement, David sang a song to the Lord.

*In the midst of feelings of impatience, David chose to focus on the goodness of God.

What a model David is for all Christians! Christians are not people who never have doubts. In fact, it could be argued that doubts actually reveal the reality of faith. Christians are not people who never feel abandoned. Christians are not people who never have fears. Christians are not people who never become discouraged or depressed.

But Christians are people who know God. Christians are people who have trusted in the Lord Jesus Christ and therefore have a living, personal relationship with God. Christians are people who have the ability to rise above their feelings of the moment for they know that their feelings are not always the true measure of reality. Christians are those who can trust in a Sovereign God knowing that he is able to build character and strength into their lives even through adversity. So Christians are people who have the ability to be patient even when tempted towards impatience.

People in general love to complain about the weather. As I am writing this book, I am sitting in Fred Jenkin's Florida home in February. Back home, in Rockford, Michigan where I am a pastor, the weather is totally different from Lake Placid, Florida. Today, as I am writing this chapter, it is fifteen degrees in Rockford. Right now I am enjoying eighty degrees on Fred's sun porch. How thankful I am for Fred's gracious generosity in letting me use his Florida winter home to write this book. When I call my son, Justin, who is the Student Ministries Pastor at our church back home in Michigan, he complains about the winter weather (and I admit that I love to rub it in a bit). But he knows that complaining about the weather is really a fruitless hobby because no amount of complaining is going to change the weather. Still it's a fun hobby for many to gripe about the weather in Michigan where four seasons can be experienced in one day.

As more and more research is being done, experts are finding that the aspect of the weather that has the most effect on us is light. When the daylight is shortened in the winter, when we go for long periods of time with the skies being overcast, when we are cooped up in a house or office for days out of the sunlight, we have a greater tendency towards feeling down or depressed. We have a syndrome called SAD (Seasonal Affective Disorder) that has been coined in an attempt to describe the negative effects that a lack of sunlight can have on us. There are even special lights that are being marketed now that we can sit under in an attempt to lift our spirits.

Now a person might go outside on an overcast, cloudy day and feel somewhat downcast. After all, he can't see the sun in the sky. He can't feel the sun's warmth. He can't see his shadow on the ground behind him. But that person would be considered very foolish, even irrational, if he allowed his feelings to cause him to doubt the existence of the sun. Just because he can't see the sun for the clouds, just because he can't feel the sun's warmth on his skin, just because he can't see the evidence of the sun reflected in his shadow doesn't mean that the sun has ceased to exist. The sun is still out there. And if he could be lifted above the clouds in an airplane, he would see the sun shining just as brightly as ever. So even though we might feel discouraged or down, the sun is still doing its job, warming the earth and sustaining our lives. And there will come a time when the clouds will separate and we will be able to see the sunshine clearly and feel the warmth of the sun on our skin again.

So it is with our relationship with God. There will be times when we don't feel his presence. David reflected one of those times in this Psalm. David was a spiritually-minded person. He was a man whom God chose to write a good portion of the Bible. He became the king of Israel. Yet David experienced times of impatience, when he felt like God had abandoned him, when he felt like God wasn't moving fast enough in his life. But David was also a person who learned a very important spiritual lesson. David learned that his feelings were not always a barometer of reality. That just because he didn't feel God's presence didn't mean that God had ceased to exist. That just because he didn't feel that God cared about him didn't mean that God didn't hear and answer his prayers. That just because life wasn't moving fast enough for him didn't mean that God wasn't fulfilling his purposes in his life.

So David chose to trust in God's unfailing love. David chose to believe God's promises to be true and rejoice in his deliverance even before it had occurred. David chose to wait upon the Lord even when feeling impatient, realizing that one day the clouds would separate and the sunshine would be clearly visible again.

Even though Michelangelo lived almost five hundred years ago, he is still considered one of the greatest artists who ever walked on this planet. His marble sculpture of David that stands over fourteen feet tall is breath-taking to behold. His fresco on the ceiling of the Sistine Chapel where he had to lay on his back on scaffolding for almost four years continues to attract millions of visitors every year. Michelangelo's versatility as a painter, sculptor, poet and architect makes him a primary contender for the model Renaissance person along with Leonardo DaVinci.

One day a friend visited Michelangelo's studio. The artist took time to introduce the friend to many of his ongoing projects. Several months passed and the friend dropped by the studio to visit Michelangelo again. As he looked around, the friend remarked that the artist had not been able to make further progress on a certain sculpture that had caught the friend's eye the first time. *Oh no, no,* Michelangelo protested. *Look at how I rounded the arm here and smoothed out a rough edge over there and put more expression into the face.* Somewhat embarrassed, the friend backed off and said that he had meant major progress and not such little things. Michelangelo then made a famous and wise observation. *It's the little thing that is needed to make perfection, and perfection is no little thing.*

God has committed himself to the perfection of each and every one of his children. The Apostle Paul wrote to the church of Philippi that we can be confident in the fact that the same God who began a good work of grace in our lives will not be satisfied until he completes it. (Phil. 1:6) As God is knocking off an edge here or sanding a rough spot over there, it might not appear that much is being accomplished. We might become impatient and wonder why God is taking so long? But God is at work. As the ultimate creator and master artist, we need to trust him to complete that work he has started in our lives, even though it might take longer than we think it should.

GOD'S PRESENCE IN SUFFERING
Chapter 7

Wil was a pitiful sight. He was only eighteen years of age, but he had lost the will to live. Only a couple of years before, Wil had been a young man with great dreams and a bright future. He was a brilliant student in literature, math, history and the arts. He had been a gifted athlete playing baseball, football and hockey at school. He was a committed Christian. He had even sensed God's leading in his life to go into the ministry. In fact, Wil had applied and been accepted at Yale Divinity School. But then, in March of Wil's senior year, one event happened that started a downward spiral in Wil's life.

He was playing on his school hockey team against Army. One of his opponents swung his hockey stick back by mistake and smashed Wil in the mouth. Almost all of his teeth were knocked out as his mouth was suddenly a mass of bloody pulp. Wil was rushed to the hospital where he received stitches and his wounds were cleaned and dressed. But Wil's problems didn't stop there. As he was recovering at home from his mouth injury, he started to have some stomach disorders. When he went back to the doctor for his stomach problems, the doctor found an irregular heartbeat. Fearing that any strenuous activity would now affect his erratic heart, the doctor confined Wil to complete bed rest. Within just a few months, Wil had gone from being a star athlete and gifted student with the brightest future ahead of him to being a semi-invalid confined to his home. There would be no more sports, probably no more school. Wil's mind became obsessed with one thought day and night, the thought that he was going to die young. And his spirits plunged into the depths of despair.

Eight years passed. Wil was now just a shadow of the person that he had been before. Gone was any optimism; gone was any joy in his life; his life was now defined by degrees of suffering.

All the time that Wil was going through this dark period of suffering in his life, his younger brother was standing by watching helplessly, praying for wisdom as to how to support the one he loved so much. Finally, he got an idea. He came to Wil and suggested a joint business venture. Maybe it was true that Wil couldn't be physically strenuous anymore, but he still had that keen mind. If Wil would be the brains of the outfit, he, the younger brother, would handle most of the physical labor. Wil thought about the offer and finally decided to accept it. Today, we are all happy that he did, for few people have changed our lifestyles as much as Wil and his younger brother. For as Wil became involved in this business venture with his younger brother, his spirits began to lift and finally to soar. And Wil took a whole nation and even the world up with him. For those two brothers first set up a small bicycle shop. But eventually, Wilbur and Orville Wright grew in their technological skills until they invented the first airplane. And now, amazingly, we can go to an airport, board a plane and in a few hours fly to a place where it would have taken people in the Wright's day years to travel to. But few people today remember that this life-changing invention of the airplane that we take for granted today was born out of intense, deep, even suicidal suffering.

One of the most difficult lessons that anybody learns in life is the fact that a certain amount of suffering is indispensable to ultimate success for there are lessons learned in suffering that cannot be learned in any other way. One of the most intriguing verses in the entire Bible is found in Hebrews 2:10 where it says of the Lord Jesus Christ, *in bringing many sons to glory, it was fitting that God, for whom and through whom everything exists, should make the author of their salvation perfect through suffering.* The word *perfect* in this verse means *complete or fully mature.* Here in this amazing verse we see the fact that suffering was not optional for Jesus Christ, the Son of God. It was absolutely necessary. For even though he was the perfect human, the sinless Son of God, there were certain areas of his life that would have not been completed unless he experienced suffering. So Jesus Christ, the author of our salvation, had to suffer for he was made perfect or complete through suffering.

So it should not surprise us at all to find intense periods of suffering in the life of David. We have previously seen his exile from his home and his family running from the threatening sword of King Saul. Certainly this was a time of intense suffering. God was in the process of making David into a man of great character who would be an influential king and leader of his people. Suffering was needed in this process.

Nor should it surprise us when God allows suffering to enter our lives. Nobody is immune to suffering. A measure of suffering is needed in each of our lives to teach lessons that cannot be learned in any other way. So, like David, we are wise if we cooperate with God in learning the lessons in suffering that we need to learn, lessons that help to complete and perfect our character.

Psalm 22 is one of David's most important works. David was obviously enduring great suffering when he composed this Psalm. But whether he consciously knew it or not, David was also writing prophetically of the atoning death of the Lord Jesus Christ for no fewer than a dozen specific prophecies were fulfilled from this Psalm when

Jesus walked up that hill called Golgotha and gave his life as a sin sacrifice for us. In fact, it was this very Psalm that was in the mind and on the lips of Jesus as he hung upon the cross.

This Psalm reveals at least **three types of suffering** that David endured (and that Christ endured to an even greater degree). We all will also endure these types of suffering to some degree. The comfort that David found when enduring these kinds of suffering can provide great solace and encouragement to each of us. Because of the prophetic nature of this Psalm, it is also important to remember the atoning work of our Savior on the cross as we work through this passage.

First of all, David speaks of the feelings of isolation and loneliness that often accompany suffering in our lives.

My God, my God, why have you forsaken me? Why are you so far from saving me, so far from the words of my groaning? O my God, I cry out by day, but you do not answer, by night, and am not silent. (Psalm 22:1,2)

We don't know the exact historical setting of this Psalm. Most Bible scholars feel that it was composed during the time of David's exile while he was on the run from King Saul. Many feel that the specific setting for this Psalm is found in 1 Samuel 30. David and his men had offered to join King Achish of Gath in battle. Achish wanted David to come along, but God had moved in the hearts of the other Philistine rulers to halt this plan so that David would not have to join the Philistines in battle against King Saul and the Israelite army. Obviously, if David would have fought in a victorious battle with the Philistines over the Israelites, this could have presented huge problems to him later when the Israelites were considering whether to make him king or not. It would be very difficult to anoint a person to be your king when he had joined with your enemy in defeating you. God worked it out so David would never be faced with this dilemma by moving in the Philistine leaders' hearts to reject David and his men from their assault. So David and his men were sent back to Ziklag where they and their families were living, secure in Philistine land from the hand of Saul. But when David led his men back to Ziklag, he found the worst possible scenario. Some Amalekites had raided the town where they had been living in their absence and had taken all of their families and possessions. Understandably, David's men were beside themselves with anger and grief having lost all of their families and possessions to the Amalekites, and they turned their venom on their leader, David. 1 Samuel 30:6 records David's dilemma: *David was greatly distressed because the men were talking of stoning him; each one was bitter in spirit because of his sons and daughters. But David found strength in the Lord his God.*

This was undoubtedly one of the lowest points in David's life. He had already experienced rejection from King Saul and the recognized leaders of Israel. He had just been rejected by the Philistines as they didn't value his fighting abilities enough to want him in battle with them. He comes back to Ziklag to find that his family and all of his possessions had been confiscated by the Amalekites. And now his formerly loyal men whom he had trained and who had fought beside him were in the process of revolting against him. They were plotting to take his life by stoning him. It just couldn't get any worse than this. You can see why David would cry out in anguish: *My God, My God, why have you forsaken me?* I feel so all alone. I feel so isolated. I feel so forsaken.

As forsaken as David felt during this low period in his life, there is another example in history of one who felt even more forsaken. For this individual not only had his enemies turned on him and his formerly loyal friends leave him, but he also experienced more than just the threat of execution. This individual was being executed by the cruelest and most painful method practiced at the time. It was as the Lord Jesus Christ was hanging upon the cross of Calvary, paying for our sins as God's atoning sacrifice that the final and most painful rejection of all occurred. As Jesus Christ was becoming sin for us, his holy and righteous Father could not maintain fellowship with him. God the Father had to turn his back on his one and only Son. David might have felt forsaken by God but in reality God never did forsake David. And the prophet Samuel records that he ultimately found strength in the Lord his God. But God did have to turn his back on his Son as he hung upon the cross of Calvary. Is it any wonder that these words were on the lips of Jesus as one of the seven phrases that he uttered from the cross? *My God, my God, why have you forsaken me?* Both Matthew and Mark record Christ's painful question in their gospel accounts. *(Matthew 27:46 & Mark 15:34)*

What can a person do when he or she experiences the suffering of feeling isolated and forsaken? David found a comfort that he expressed in the next three verses, a comfort that undoubtedly was the only solace that Jesus Christ had on that hill called Golgotha.

Yet you are enthroned as the Holy One; you are the praise of Israel. In you our fathers put their trust; they trusted and you delivered them. They cried to you and were saved; in you they trusted and were not disappointed. (Psalm 22:3-5)

It doesn't matter how painful or threatening a situation might be, God has not abdicated his throne. In spite of David feeling so isolated and alone, God was still directing his life. God had already protected him from fighting against his own kinsmen with the Philistines, and he was going to not only help David recover his possessions and family as well as the possessions and families of the rest of his men, but he was also going to use this occasion to remove the Amalekites as a future threat.

David needed to remember that God had delivered many of his forefathers from worse situations in the past. God had taken the whole Jewish nation out of the bondage of Egyptian slavery in a manner that was simply miraculous. God had delivered his people in the past, and he would certainly be faithful to David now in his predicament.

We can only imagine the comfort that this passage brought to the mind and heart of the Lord Jesus as he was undergoing his execution. For while our Savior only quoted the first verse, it is clear that this entire Psalm was in his mind and on his heart. True, the situation appeared to be bleak. This was the moment when the Prince of Darkness was gloating. Yet God the Father was still on the throne. And just as he had delivered his people in the past, so he would not forsake His Holy One or leave his body to decay in the tomb. Just as God would work this low point in David's life out for his good, so God would bring about the greatest blessing for the human race through the apparently tragic death of his one and only Son. Because the Lord Jesus Christ died, we now have the opportunity to live for all eternity.

If God met his servant David in his time of need, and if God brought eternal good out of the suffering of his one and only Son, can't the God who never leaves his sovereign throne also meet us in our times of need?

David went on to reveal a **second kind of suffering** that he experienced in the next three verses. These were the feelings of low self-esteem and rejection that he endured.

But I am a worm and not a man, scorned by men and despised by the people. All who see me mock me; they hurl insults, shaking their heads: "He trusts in the LORD; let the LORD rescue him. Let him deliver him, since he delights in him." (Psalm 22:6-8)

One of the natural consequences of feeling isolated and alone is feeling worthless, having a loss of self-esteem. When we feel that everyone has rejected us, we don't even feel like we deserve to be a part of the human race. Here David testified that he didn't even feel human. He admitted that he felt like a *worm and not a man*. His men were mocking him; they were ridiculing him; they were picking up stones and threatening him with them.

But it is most interesting to note how David's feelings were prophetic and even more fully fulfilled in the suffering that the Lord Jesus Christ endured. The word that is translated *worm* here is the very same word that is also translated *crimson* in Isaiah 1:18 where it says, *"Come now, let us reason together," says the Lord. "Though your sins are like scarlet, they shall be as white as snow; though they are red as crimson, they shall be like wool."*

There are a couple of Hebrew words that could be translated *worm*. But this specific one that David chooses here describes a small grub like worm that was used in making a very valuable red dye. This dye was literally made by taking these *towla* worms and crushing them.

Out of these worms being crushed like grapes the valuable crimson-red dye was secured. This dye was used in making many of the royal garments.

What a picture this is of what transpired on the cross of Calvary. The Bible says that it was the Father's will to crush his son. (Isaiah 53:10) As the very lifeblood flowed from the hands, feet and side of the Lord Jesus, he was like this *towla* worm. A priceless dye was brought forth that would once and for all cover our sins. But the blessing that Christ's death was producing in no way minimizes the sufferings he endured. Jesus Christ suffered the indignation being dehumanized like a worm, the suffering of being looked upon, scorned, mocked and insulted as one whom people were regarding as less than human.

What was David's comfort as he was suffering the loss of self-esteem and rejection? What was Christ's comfort as he reflected upon these words on the cross of Calvary?

Yet you brought me out of the womb; you made me trust in you even at my mother's breast. From birth I was cast upon you; from my mother's womb you have been my God. (Psalm 22:9,10)

David realized that none of the mocking, ridiculing men around him had anything to do with his existence. In fact, no human being can ultimately give us life. Yes, it is true that our mothers and fathers were instrumental in the birth process. But the Bible is clear when it says that God is ultimately the author of life. God is the one who gives life to that union of sperm and egg. And when God creates something, he pronounces it to be good. When

God makes a human being, no one has the power to dehumanize it.

What a thrilling thought this must have been to the Lord Jesus Christ as he hung upon the cross! Here he was being dehumanized by the mocking crowds around him. They were spitting upon him; they were hurling insults at him. But in his mind he must have gone back to this Psalm as he hung upon that tree. He must have seen how even those insults were fulfilling God's prophecy. And he might also have gone back to his own miraculous birth, born of the virgin Mary. If God the Holy Spirit had overshadowed the virgin Mary so that she might be enabled to conceive the very Son of God himself, who among this mocking and ridiculing crowd had the power or authority to declare him to be less than human. It is God and God alone who is the giver and sustainer of life.

One of the major goals of the educators in our nation today is to build self-esteem into the lives of our young people. Yet in spite of all of the efforts and billions of dollars that are being funneled towards this purpose, young people and adults alike continue to struggle with feelings of poor self-esteem and rejection. But when a person comes to grips with the singular fact that God and God alone has given life to make a human being in his own image and likeness, it really doesn't matter anymore what others might think. Peer pressure loses its grip when confronted with this powerful and freeing truth.

A **third type of suffering** that David endured was his physical pain.

Many bulls surround me; strong bulls of Bashan encircle me. Roaring lions tearing their prey open their mouths wide against me. I am poured out like water, and all my bones are out of joint. My heart has turned to wax;

it has melted away within me. My strength is dried up like a potsherd, and my tongue sticks to the roof of my mouth; you lay me in the dust of death. Dogs have surrounded me; a band of evil men has encircled me, they have pierced my hands and my feet. I can count all my bones; people stare and gloat over me. They divide my garments among them and cast lots for my clothing. (Psalm 22:12-18)

It is obvious that David is speaking figuratively here for there is no record of any experience in his life that would approximate what he is describing in these verses. David is describing an execution in these verses and we know he never had to suffer that literally. We are given the Biblical record of David's death as he passed away peacefully in his bed at *a good old age, having enjoyed long life, wealth and honor (1 Chronicles 29:28).* But we all recognize that emotional and spiritual suffering can bring even physical torment to our bodies. And it is likely that David was enduring some agonizing times when he wrote these words. Perhaps he was even suffering some physical symptoms.

But isn't it amazing how the Holy Spirit guided David to literally describe the physical sufferings that the Lord Jesus Christ would endure upon the cross of Calvary? His **bones being jerked out of joint** which was the natural consequence of crucifixion. For when the condemned was nailed to the cross while still on the ground and that cross was then lifted to an upright position and dropped into its slot in the earth with a thud, the arms were normally jerked right out of their sockets. **The severe thirst that was caused by the loss of bodily fluids**. As the blood drained from the body, the dehydrating flesh would cry out for water, liquids to replenish the system. Some experts in this area claim that the severe thirst was

94

actually among the greatest of all the sufferings endured by the one being crucified. That nagging desire for water that never went away. In fact, the only personal complaint that Jesus uttered in his seven phrases from the cross was *I thirst*. **The hands and feet that were pierced.** This was unique to Roman persecution. Before crucifixion, there wasn't another means of execution that would pierce both hands and feet. Yet, amazingly, David wrote these words a thousand years before Christ died upon the cross. **People staring and gloating at his naked body.** One of the most humiliating aspects of Roman crucifixion was the fact that the condemned was forced to hang naked at a busy intersection before a gawking and mocking world. This was especially humbling for the Jewish people who valued modesty so highly. Details, even to the point of predicting **the gambling for his clothing** were given by David. The physical sufferings that the Lord Jesus Christ endured in his atoning death were intense beyond measure.

Where can any comfort be found when intense physical suffering enters one's life?

But you, O LORD, be not far off; O my Strength, come quickly to help me. Deliver my life from the sword, my precious life from the power of the dogs. Rescue me from the mouth of the lions; save me from the horns of the wild oxen. I will declare your name to my brothers; in the congregation I will praise you. You who fear the LORD, praise him! All you descendants of Jacob, honor him! Revere him, all you descendants of Israel! For he has not despised or disdained the suffering of the afflicted one; he has not hidden his face from him but has listened to his cry for help. (Psalm 22:19-24)

God did not desert his servant David. Yes, the situation appeared to be hopeless. But God restored David's possessions and family and, in just a short time, David would be the king of Judah and then Israel.

Nor did God desert his one and only Son, Jesus Christ. Yes, the situation on the cross appeared to be hopeless. But in reality, sin and death were being defeated and God's arch enemy was being crushed. In just three short days, there would be new life and hope realized forever because of Christ's death, burial and resurrection from the grave.

Nor will God ever desert any of his children. It doesn't matter how severe the suffering might be, it doesn't matter what kind of suffering it might be, God will never despise or disdain the sufferings of his children, but has committed himself to come to their aid and even bring blessing out of their sufferings.

So God's children can take heart even in the midst of their sufferings. God brought his servant David through his suffering; God brought his one and only Son through his suffering; and God brought great blessing to all of our lives through their sufferings. So we can have the confidence that God will not desert us during our times of need. And God can also bring great blessing through our sufferings as well.

STOOPING TO GREATNESS
Chapter 8

The most decorated American war hero in World War 2 was Audie Murphy. He was wounded three times in battle; he was credited with personally taking out two hundred and forty of the enemy soldiers; of the two hundred and thirty-five men in his beginning company, he was one of only two who survived the war; he was awarded twenty-seven medals by the time the conflict was over including three from the French and one from Belgium.

All this was achieved by a young man who was one of eleven children of a Texas sharecropper, a young man who actually lied about his age so that he could join the army at the age of seventeen. Nobody could have predicted that Audie Murphy would become such an outstanding soldier.

Predictably, Audie Murphy was swept away to Hollywood following World War 2 where he became an instant celebrity and movie star. He played himself alongside James Cagney in the movie version of his autobiography. In just a short while, he had earned more than two and a half million dollars acting in pictures. Life couldn't have been better for this young man in his mid-twenties who was idolized by everyone as a war hero and rich beyond his wildest imaginations.

But while Audie Murphy was courageous in the heat of battle, he couldn't seem to cope with success as well. Within a decade after his first hit movie, Murphy was almost destitute. He was forced to declare bankruptcy as a pauper. So when he died in a plane crash in the wooded mountains of Virginia in what should have been the prime of his life, the obituaries mercifully focused on what he had been, not on what he had become.

Many people fail to reach their potential in life because of the discouragement of failures. They give it their best shot in life and they fail. So disheartened by their shortcomings, they just give up and quit setting any goals for themselves in the future. It is critical for a person to learn to deal with failure in a positive manner if ultimate success is to be attained, for everyone fails at times in life.

But there are other people who demonstrate the ability to rise to the challenge of failure who cannot handle success. They have the perseverance to get up and try again after failing, to endure trials and troubles. But then when they finally achieve their goal, they can't handle the success that they have achieved. They leave behind the positive character traits that brought them success and begin to coast downward. Their final end is often worse than their beginning. How many people are there who stay on track as long as they are pursuing their goal only to fall apart after they attain success? Athletes who finally make it to the professional ranks, but then ruin themselves with alcohol or drugs. Businessmen who finally get that position with the company, but then have their families fall apart. Christian workers who get their eyes off of Christ and fall into some kind of sin that cripples their service for the Lord.

David was a man who learned how to handle success successfully. No one can make the claim that he was perfect. Subsequent chapters are going to focus on periods in his life when he endured spiritual weakness. But David was a man who was generally able to handle success as well as failure.

David experienced humble beginnings. He was the youngest of the eight sons of Jesse. Of all the Jesse boys, he was the least likely to be voted as the most likely to succeed. The older boys were brave soldiers, but David was the one who was given the job of watching the sheep out on the Bethlehem hillsides. But David had great potential, and he honed skills that would be useful to him in the future rather than frittering away his time. David practiced his sharp shooting with the sling until he had the confidence to face the Philistine giant, Goliath, and take him down with one shot hitting a couple inch square target on the dead run. David developed his musical abilities playing his home-made harp until he became the palace musician, playing the soothing melodies needed to quiet the king's troubled spirits.

And then when that most difficult period entered David's life, when King Saul in his madness turned on him, venting all of his anger and frustrations, chasing him all around the countryside trying to kill him, David persevered and endured with integrity. He trusted in the Lord and waited upon him. He did not strike back taking matters into his own hands when he had the opportunity to do so. But he rather developed his leadership skills, amassing around him a formidable force of skilled and courageous soldiers so that he would be ready when his time came.

Very often in life we find that when God is ready to act, he acts quickly. Sometimes we have to be patient and wait a long time until God's timing is right. But when God's perfect time comes, critical events can happen in a hurry. This was certainly the case for David. For more than a decade, David was on the run from King Saul. It must have seemed at times like this difficult period in his life would never end. But he learned many lessons during this time that we have looked at in previous chapters from some of the Psalms that he wrote.   When David learned all of those lessons that God had planned for him, God acted decisively to fulfill the promise that he had made to David through the Prophet Samuel who anointed him with the oil of kingship.

In one battle with the Philistines, King Saul and his son, Jonathan, who would have been the assumed heir to the throne in the eyes of the people, were both killed. Suddenly, the nation of Israel was leaderless.

It would have been most natural for Judah to turn to David for leadership.   After all, David was born and raised around the Judean town of Bethlehem. David had been the heir anointed by the respected prophet, Samuel. David had really been the one who had been protecting the families in Judah from the Philistines during the later part of Saul's reign anyway. Yet it took the northern tribes of Israel seven more years to recognize David as their king after they saw his stellar abilities as a leader outlasting the feeble attempts of Ish-Bosheth, one of Saul's other sons, to establish a throne.

The Philistines were certainly not going to stand by and allow David to assume the throne unopposed. After all, they had the Israelites right where they wanted them now. They had just defeated the Israeli army in battle. King Saul and his oldest son, Jonathan, were both dead. They wanted Israel to be without any recognized leadership so that they would be easier to control. But the Philistines soon found that they were dealing with an entirely different military strategist when they came to oppose David.

The Philistine's strength was in their chariots and iron weapons. The Bible clearly states that the Philistines recognized this advantage and wouldn't allow the Israelites to even have a blacksmith in their territory.

Not a blacksmith could be found in the whole land of Israel, because the Philistines had said, "Otherwise the Hebrews will make swords or spears." So all Israel went down to the Philistines to have their plowshares, mattocks, axes and sickles sharpened. The price was two thirds of a shekel for sharpening plowshares and mattocks, and a third of a shekel for sharpening forks and axes and for repointing goads. (1 Samuel 13:19-21)

It was really the chariot that had perfected the iron artillery for the Philistines. They would fasten swords to the wheels of the chariots and mow through the opposing armies as if they were harvesting wheat. The Israelites were quite helpless against this superior weaponry. And Saul, for all of his courage and valor, had not shown himself to be a wise military strategist.

The typical battle against the Philistines would begin with the enemy assembling their chariots in a large plain such as the Valley of Jezreel where Saul finally lost his life. The Philistines would then call the Israelite army down to fight against them. That is what Goliath was doing when David came to visit his brothers on the battle lines. Saul would dutifully lead the Israelite soldiers down onto the battle field where his army would be routed by the superior weaponry of the Philistines. And this scene took place time and time again during the Kingship of Saul.

But when David became king, the scene changed and changed rapidly. Immediately, the Philistines assembled their chariots in the valley of Rephaim and called David down to fight as recorded in 2 Samuel 5. But David was not foolish enough to fight the Philistines on their home court. David had learned how to fight in the hill country while fleeing from Saul. He had trained his men in this different type of guerilla fighting. In essence,

David said to the Philistines, *if you want to fight me, you come to Baal Perazim and I'll be waiting for you.* The Philistines were in a corner now. They felt the need to stop this budding monarchy, but David would not fight them on the plain where they had the distinct advantage. The Philistines chose to come up to fight against David and his men. This turned out to be a huge mistake for them. In two quick and decisive battles, David routed the Philistine armies and confirmed his control of the hill country. Finally, the Israelites were free from their fears of the Philistines.

David then captured the mountain city of Jerusalem from the Jebusites, making it his capital. It was a perfect, neutral site being right near the border of Judah and Israel. David then brought the Ark of the Covenant to Jerusalem and set up the tabernacle, thereby unifying the country religiously. And within just a short time, David had accomplished what Saul hadn't been able to do in his entire lifetime. David had freed the Israelites from the threat of the Philistines and he had established a capital city where God could be honored and worshipped. From this base of control, David could then start to defeat the surrounding countries one at a time until he was in control over the whole Middle Eastern region. There haven't been many clearer examples of military success in all of the world's history than that of David who took a nation from being the doormat of a tribal bully to being the ruling power of an entire region of the world in just a short period of time.

So we are coming into a completely different period in the life of David when we come to Psalm 18. We don't know exactly when this Psalm was written, but we do know that it was after Saul was dead, after David had assumed the throne and after he had subdued the threats of his surrounding enemies. It could have been written later in his reign for there is a passage in 2 Samuel 22 that closely parallels this Psalm. But we can be sure that this Psalm was written after David had become king.

Psalm 18 is a song of praise and thanksgiving to the Lord. It is a rather lengthy Psalm containing fifty verses; most of the Psalms are shorter than this one. In this Psalm, David glories in the power of God to deliver him from all of his foes.

There are several verses right in the middle of this Psalm that give a clue to three characteristics of David that enabled him to handle his successes so successfully. These characteristics are his **authenticity**, his **humility** and his **faith**. Conversely, the lack of these characteristics is the major reason why so many people fail to handle success well.

To the faithful you show yourself faithful, to the blameless you show yourself blameless, to the pure you show yourself pure, but to the crooked you show yourself shrewd. (Psalm 18:25,26)

When we first read these words, we are somewhat surprised. We might even get the wrong impression of what David is saying here unless we are careful. David is not claiming to be absolutely faithful, blameless and pure here. David is not even saying that a person must become pure and blameless in order to have any initial relationship with God. He is not saying that a person must clean up his or her life in order to be acceptable to God, that a person must first become faithful to God before God will be faithful to him, that a person must first present God with a blameless life before God will accept him, that a person must first purify himself before God will show himself to be pure. The Bible is very clear that we are not accepted by God because of what we do to please him, but rather we are accepted by God on the basis of his mercy and grace, by what he has done for us so that we might be acceptable to him. David hadn't been chosen by God because he was powerful and mighty. He knew this. David was just a young shepherd when Samuel first anointed him to be king. Jesse had to call his youngest son in from the fields where he was tending the flocks.

And the remainder of this Psalm and the historical context in which it was written demonstrate the fact that David realized and accepted the grace of God in his life. We must always remember that David was writing as a believer in God here. He was not writing as one who was becoming a believer in God. The Bible tells us that we are saved only by God's grace, not by any good works that we do. *For it is by grace that you are saved through faith, and that not of yourselves, it is the gift of God. Not by works lest anyone should boast. (Ephesians 2:8,9)* When David had brought the Ark of the Covenant into Jerusalem, he had done so with much sacrificing. 2 Samuel 6 records that every six steps David stopped the procession of the ark to sacrifice a bull and a calf. David was acutely aware of his sin and the sins of the people, and he realized his need for God's cleansing of those sins.

But having acknowledged the fact that we are not born again into God's family by being blameless or righteous in our own strength, we must not overlook the fact that our continuing relationship with God must be on the basis of authenticity. God is a God of truth. That is one of God's never-changing attributes. Therefore, anyone who is going to have a living relationship with God must have one on the basis of truthfulness.

One of the dangers that success brings with it is the danger of a person starting to play a role, forgetting his

104

roots, and pretending to be someone that he really isn't on the inside. Saul fell for that temptation. He started out well, but soon fell into the temptation of thinking that he was more important than he really was. That was the reason for the Prophet Samuel reminding him that he was a man who had come from humble roots in 1 Samuel 15:17. That was one of the reasons why God rejected Saul. A God of truth cannot have a living relationship with someone who is playing a role, living a life of hypocrisy.

David never forgot who he was. He remained authentic to himself, before his people and with God. He recognized the fact that a person must come to God with a trusting, innocent and pure heart if he is to have a living relationship with God. No human being can ever fool God. God is omniscient. God knows even the innermost secrets of our hearts. If we try to trick God, we will find him to be shrewder than we can ever be. The Lord Jesus Christ himself echoed a similar message in the sixth beatitude in his Sermon on the Mount when he said, *blessed are the pure in heart, for they shall see God.*

A **second characteristic** that David revealed in this passage is humility.

You save the humble but bring low those whose eyes are haughty. (Psalm 18:27)

There is an account that Samuel gave of David's life that illustrates David's authenticity and humility very clearly in contrast to the kingly theater that Saul tried to play. This is the account of David supervising the bringing of the Ark into Jerusalem found in 2 Samuel 6. David, of course, had failed to bring the Ark into the capital city on his first try. He had tried to carry the Ark in the same manner that the Philistines had returned the Ark back to the Israelites. The Philistines, not knowing about God's law or commandments given from Mt. Sinai, just wanted to get rid of the Ark because of the plague that it had brought upon them. They had realized their error in taking the Ark from the Israelites in the first place. So they put the Ark on a wooden cart drawn by two oxen. Then they sent the Ark away without a human driver. They were undoubtedly hoping that the cart would fall off a cliff of the precipitous roads that connected their territory with the Israelites. They even used two oxen that had never been yoked before and that had just given birth to new calves to pull the cart. They undoubtedly hoped that these oxen would pull the ark to its destruction.

It could be argued that the Philistines didn't know any better. They didn't have God's law. They wouldn't have known the detailed instructions as to how the Ark of the Covenant was to be carried. So God overlooked their ignorance and brought the Ark back to its homeland without incident.

But when David tried to move the Ark into Jerusalem using a cart, he should have known better. He should have consulted the priests and learned that God's prescribed method of carrying the Ark of the Covenant was by Levites carrying the long poles running through the golden rings on the sides of the Ark on their shoulders so that there would never be a risk of the Ark falling or anybody touching the Ark personally. By slipping the long poles through the rings on the sides of the Ark, the Levites would never have to touch the Ark of the Covenant. And by carrying the poles on their shoulders, they could navigate over the uneven terrain with the Ark securely fastened to the poles.

By carrying the Ark on a cart, David put both it and the attendants who were surrounding it in grave danger.

And sure enough, when the oxen stumbled and the Ark tipped dangerously, Uzzah put out his hand to steady the Ark so that it wouldn't fall off the cart. But when Uzzah touched the Ark of the Covenant, he was immediately killed by the Lord. At first, David was angry. Hadn't Uzzah just been trying to protect the Ark? Why would God strike him dead? But after he cooled down and realized the error of his own ways, David planned to move the Ark again – this time God's way.

Now King David was told, "The LORD has blessed the household of Obed-Edom and everything he has, because of the ark of God." So David went down and brought up the ark of God from the house of Obed-Edom to the City of David with rejoicing. When those who were carrying the ark of the LORD had taken six steps, he sacrificed a bull and a fattened calf. David, wearing a linen ephod, danced before the LORD with all his might, while he and the entire house of Israel brought up the ark of the LORD with shouts and the sound of trumpets.

As the ark of the LORD was entering the City of David, Michal daughter of Saul watched from a window. And when she saw King David leaping and dancing before the LORD, she despised him in her heart.

They brought the ark of the LORD and set it in its place inside the tent that David had pitched for it, and David sacrificed burnt offerings and fellowship offerings before the LORD. After he had finished sacrificing the burnt offerings and fellowship offerings, he blessed the people in the name of the LORD Almighty. Then he gave a loaf of bread, a cake of dates and a cake of raisins to each person in the whole crowd of Israelites, both men and women. And all the people went to their homes.

When David returned home to bless his household, Michal daughter of Saul came out to meet him and said, "How the king of Israel has distinguished himself today, disrobing in the sight of the slave girls of his servants as any vulgar fellow would!"

David said to Michal, "It was before the LORD, who chose me rather than your father or anyone from his house when he appointed me ruler over the LORD's people Israel - I will celebrate before the LORD. I will become even more undignified than this, and I will be humiliated in my own eyes. But by these slave girls you spoke of, I will be held in honor."

And Michal daughter of Saul had no children to the day of her death. (2 Samuel 6:12-23)

Now isn't this an interesting account? David had been given Michal, the daughter of Saul, as his wife as a reward for a victory over the Philistines. But, Michal, growing up in King Saul's household, had much different expectations as to how a king should act. She was used to her father always playing the kingly role with great pomp and circumstance. So when she saw David freely expressing his joy and celebration as the Ark was being brought into Jerusalem, she thought, *this is no way for a king to act.*

Now David wasn't doing anything wrong. Even though she accused him of disrobing himself, the Bible clearly says that David was wearing a linen robe. He just wasn't wearing his royal garments; he had taken off his official, kingly robe. Isn't it interesting how David responds to her? He doesn't allow her expectations that had been inbred into her by her upbringing to rob him of his freedom in expressing his praise and celebration to God.

David was comfortable being himself. That humility was pleasing to God.

There are many people who feel that they must put on the garment of spirituality before they come before God. Because they know that God is perfect in holiness and cannot look favorably upon sin, they try to hide their sins and pretend that they are sinless when they approach God. Because they know that God is perfect in his strength without any weaknesses, they try to hide their frailties and pretend that they are self-sufficient and strong when they approach God. Because they know that God is perfect in his love and grace, they try to present themselves as compassionate people when inside they might not feel that way when they approach God. Because they know that God is perfect in his forgiveness and mercy, they try to present themselves as forgiving people when inside there are feelings of anger and bitterness when they approach God.

This approach is not only ineffective, it is a great insult to God for it assumes that we have the ability to hide something from a God who is all-knowing. Our innermost thoughts and hearts are an open book before God. He knows what we are thinking; he knows what we are feeling. And, amazingly, he loves and accepts us just as we are. God desires for us to have a vibrant, personal relationship with him. But that relationship must begin with authenticity and humility. We must just be ourselves before God. We must admit our failures, confess our sins, and express our feelings openly and freely. It is only then that God will be able to give us his strength, forgive our sins and heal our wounds. David was the model of a person who was after God's own heart. And that model is seen so clearly when he supervised the bringing of the Ark into Jerusalem.

David was not only authentic and humble, but he was also trusting. **David was a man of faith in God.**

You, O LORD, keep my lamp burning; my God turns my darkness into light. With your help I can advance against a troop; with my God I can scale a wall. As for God, his way is perfect; the word of the LORD is flawless. He is a shield for all who take refuge in him. For who is God besides the LORD? And who is the Rock except our God? It is God who arms me with strength and makes my way perfect. He makes my feet like the feet of a deer; he enables me to stand on the heights. He trains my hands for battle; my arms can bend a bow of bronze. You give me your shield of victory, and your right hand sustains me; you stoop down to make me great. You broaden the path beneath me, so that my ankles do not turn. (Psalm 18:28-36)

There is one phrase in this passage that is simply amazing to me. Every time I read this Psalm, this phrase just jumps out and grabs my attention. It is the last phrase in verse 35 where David said of God, ***you stoop down to make me great.***

What a summary of what God has done for us! From David's perspective, he saw a God who took the most unobvious person and made him to be King of Israel. David had been a shepherd boy, the youngest member of his family. Samuel certainly hadn't been impressed with David at first. God, are you sure this is the person you want me to anoint? But God, in the richness of his grace, took this young man and made him to be a king.

Today, we can see this truth in an even greater way from our perspective. As the second person of the Triune Godhead left the glories of heaven to come into this world, emptying himself and taking upon himself the form of a servant, being born not in a palace but in a stable, is it not true that God has stooped down to make us great? The Lord Jesus Christ came so that we could be redeemed and adopted into the family of God as full heirs of God's riches. The Son of God became a human being so that we as human beings could become sons of God. Certainly God has stooped down so that we could become great.

David saw this pattern in God and David modeled it in his own life. That was what made David the king that Saul could never become. So it can be in each of our lives. Just as God has stooped down to make us great, so he desires for each of us to be authentic, humble, and people who believe and trust God so that, through our service to others, we further the growth of God's kingdom and also grow in our relationship with God.

Chapter 9

The year was 1780. Mr. Daly was the manager of a local theater. One Saturday night, Daly was having dinner with some of his friends. He was trying to convince his friends of the power of advertising. Daly's friends were skeptical, countering that advertising was just a waste of time and money. Well, one thing led to another and finally Mr. Daly offered a wager to his friends in an attempt to convince them of the power of advertising. Daly bet his friends that he could invent a totally meaningless word and make that word a part of the English language in just one week by using the power of advertising. Daly's friends just laughed at him. This would be the easiest money that they would ever make. So they agreed and shook hands on it. Daly had one week to make up a word and then make that word a part of the English language.

The next morning, Daly's friends were somewhat surprised to see a strange word flashed all over town. It was on billboards. It was on posters. It was in the windows of stores. And, of course, it was on the marquee of Daly's theater. Within a couple of days, people were starting to ask questions about this word. What does it mean? Where did it come from? Amazingly, Daly did make that four letter word, a word that was totally invented by him, a word that didn't have any language derivation at all, a word that didn't even have a meaning, a part of our language through the power of advertising. In fact, we still use Daly's word today. It now has a meaning, of course. In fact, Webster gives Daly's word three major meanings. One of them is *a practical joke*. But students everywhere have come to dread Daly's invention – the word *QUIZ*.

It is a fact of life that every person has many influences that help to mold and direct the course of his or her life. Advertisers count on this fact, of course. But there are many other influences that are even more powerful than advertising. Parents, teachers, friends, church leaders, community leaders, fellow workers, and many others have more influence on us than we even know. And one of the differences between people who are successful and people who flounder through life is found in the choice of influences that the person makes. Wise people choose beneficial influences in life. Wise people choose quality products over the poorer ones in advertising. Wise people choose sharpening friends over destructive ones. While it is impossible to choose every influence, wise people do their best to choose the best influences that they can and learn valuable lessons from even the poor influences that are placed in their paths. Probably the strongest influences that I had in helping me to decide what kind of coach I was going to be when I coached the Varsity Soccer team at Cornerstone University for three years were two college basketball coaches that I had. The first probably shouldn't even have been coaching basketball in the first place for basketball wasn't his primary sport. He had been a semi-professional baseball player. But he had been a good athlete so he understood the sports world and he was a tremendous motivator. His love for his players was evident. His locker room speeches became legendary. He has now passed on to Glory but I will never forget the influence that he had on me. In my sophomore year, we had another coach. He really knew a great deal more about basketball strategy than my previous coach had, but he was a hot-head. He lost his temper regularly in practice and during games. If a player made a mistake, he would yank him from the game and publicly humiliate him. I felt the sting of his venom as a player and watched many of my fellow players cringe when he came around. I learned many lessons from that coach as well and he has also had a great influence on my life. I vowed that when I coached, I would never publicly berate a player, but I would rather take him off to the side after the game was over and talk to him privately about any mistakes he had made.

One of the most important decisions that we make in life involves the influences that we will generally surround ourselves with and how we will choose to respond to potentially negative influences in our lives.

We have now entered the phase of David's life when his outlook has become much more optimistic. Saul is now dead, killed in battle with the Philistines. David no longer has the threat of Saul hunting him down hanging over his head. And David has now been anointed King of Israel. He has subdued the Philistine threat and other surrounding nations are quickly falling into line as well. Life is progressively looking very good. The future looks bright. And David's Psalms written during this period of his life reflect this more optimistic spirit. David writes in

Psalm 16, *Lord, you have assigned me my portion and my cup; you have made my lot secure. The boundary lines have fallen for me in pleasant places; surely I have a delightful inheritance. (Psalm 16:5,6)* These are the words of a man who is happy with life.

But David never forgot the influences in his life that had brought him to this place. He had learned from Saul's negative example. He remembered the lessons that Doeg the Edomite and other opportunistic evildoers had taught him. And he most of all remembered the important influences that godly people had provided in his life, the prophet Samuel, his closest friend Jonathan, Abiathar the priest who was also a close associate, and many others. David glories in his fellow followers of God who are his delight.

As for the saints who are in the land, they are the glorious ones in whom is all my delight. (Psalm 16:3)

David recognized that it was God's path of life that he would have to take if he were to continue to live life successfully. Psalm 16 reveals David's choice to follow God's path in life, to allow godly influences to direct his life. In this Psalm, as David reflects back upon God's goodness to him bringing him to this present place in his life, he recognizes God's hand in meeting all of his basic needs in life. The message that is contained in this Psalm is just as relevant today as it was three thousand years ago when it was written for every one of us still has some basic needs to be met if we are to have personal success in life.

*Life can be confusing - we all need to have direction; we all need to have help in making good decisions.   God and godly influences help to give us direction in life.

*Life can be dangerous - we all need a measure of protection to have confidence and peace of heart.   God and godly influences help to provide protection for us in life.

*Life can be lonely - we all are social creatures.   We need to feel a sense of belonging.   God and godly influences can provide fellowship for us in life.

Following God provides the direction in life.   In fact, following God is the pathway to life.   God provided direction for David in life.

I will praise the LORD, who counsels me; even at night my heart instructs me. I have set the LORD always before me. Because he is at my right hand, I will not be shaken. (Psalm 16:7,8)

Life can be confusing.   There are so many philo-sophies of life and so many who are trying to tell us what path to take.   There are so many who are trying to influence our direction in life.

Some are saying that financial security is the pathway to life.   Own a piece of the rock and you will not be shaken.   But then we see so many millionaires who are not happy people and read about others who actually take their lives in their misery and depression, and we realize that the pathway to life is not found with mere financial security.

Others tell us that being healthy is the pathway to life. Take care of your body, keep in top physical condition, eat right, exercise every day, don't smoke or drink or chew or go with girls who do - then you will find the pathway to life. But the longer we live, the more we find that no matter how much care is given to this earthly body, it still wears out. It still gets sick at times, the eyesight fails, arthritis invades the joints. This body will not last forever. No, health is not the ultimate pathway to life.

Still others tell us that relationships are the pathway to life. It's not what you accomplish but it is rather who you get to know that is most important. So build strong and intimate family relationships and cultivate strong and intimate relationships with others for this is the pathway to life. But then our parents die, and a friend turns against us, and we find that relationships are not the pathway to life.

Now, there is no doubt that financial security and health and relationships are good in themselves. If they were bad, nobody would be able to promote them as possible pathways to life with any kind of credibility. Who would believe that a life of crime or self-mutilation or total isolation is the pathway to life? But the problem comes when people try to make financial security or health or relationships or any one of a number of other good things do more than they are capable of doing. When they put too great a burden on their shoulders, they crumble under the weight because none of these is designed to be the pathway to life.

In the book of Ecclesiastes, King Solomon reflected on his struggles to find meaning and purpose in life. Solomon was a man who had every advantage possible in life. He had seemingly inexhaustible riches, wealth and financial security. He received over three hundred and twenty million dollars just in gold tribute from surrounding nations every year. That doesn't include all the money that he made from trade or silver or precious gems or tax money. He was wealthy beyond imagination. He was a man who had good health. He had every advantage to have doctors and physicians hover around him. He could eat the best tasting and most nutritious foods. There is no record that he ever had any serious illness. He died at a ripe old age for his day.

Solomon had more relationships than any of us will ever have. He had 1,000 wives. He could be friends with anyone he wanted. Everyone wanted to be Solomon's friend. Kings and queens traveled from all over the world just to get to know him. Yet Solomon found that none of these things could bring meaning to his life. He wrote, *so I hated life, because the work that is done under the sun was grievous to me. All of it is meaningless, a chasing after the wind. Eccl. 2:17*

Have you ever tried to chase the wind? I can't think of a more fruitless endeavor than trying to run after the wind. That was what life was for Solomon when he lost godly influences and direction in his life even though he had everything else life could offer.

118

Solomon's conclusion in Ecclesiastes directed him back to the only path to life. He concluded his book by writing:

Now all has been heard; here is the conclusion of the matter: Fear God and keep his commandment, for this is the whole duty of man. For God will bring every deed into judgment, including every hidden thing, whether it is good or bad. (Ecclesiastes 12:13,14)

We will never find the path to life until we listen to God's counsel and instruction. David learned that lesson; his son, Solomon, learned that lesson. So must we.

God also provided protection for David in life.

Keep me safe, O God, for in you I take refuge. . . Therefore my heart is glad and my tongue rejoices; my body also will rest secure, because you will not abandon me to the grave, nor will you let your Holy One see decay. (Psalm 16:1,9,10)

David was a man who knew what physical danger was all about. He knew what it felt like to be forced out of his home and have all of his possessions ransacked by greedy thieves. This happened to him several times in life. He knew what it felt like to try to go to sleep at night not knowing if he would wake up in the morning. He knew the terror of running for his life with skilled assassins right on his heels.

Now David did his best to protect himself. But he also knew that ultimately his protection had to come from the Lord. So David learned to rest in God for his

119

protection in life. David learned to trust in the promises of God.

We live in a paranoid world today. The American Kennel Club claims that in 1975 the most popular pure breed dog in the United States was the Poodle. There were 139,750 registered Poodles in our nation. In that year, there were only 952 registered Rottweilers. Rottweilers can be a fierce breed often used as a guard dog. Today, the Poodle population in our country has been cut in half. There are less than 60,000 registered Poodles now. Do you know how many registered Rottweilers there are now? Well over 100,000. Whereas in 1975 there were more than 139 times as many Poodles as Rottweilers, today there are about twice as many Rottweilers as there are Poodles in our country.

Today, security is one of the fastest growing businesses in our nation. Many homes have alarm systems. Most stores have security systems. You can hardly walk into any business without being photographed by a camera.

Now it is certainly the path of wisdom to take necessary precautions to protect ourselves and property. We live in a fallen world that houses many dishonest people. I often think that one of the joys of heaven will be the fact that there won't be any locks on any doors. We won't have to carry any keys with us. That means we won't lose any more keys or lock ourselves out of our cars anymore. Won't that be great? But today, we need locks and keys. We lock the doors to our church after the worship service starts. Our church has a security committee. But if we are relying on locks, alarms and security systems to provide peace of mind for us, we are going to be sadly disappointed.

I remember the time when this lesson became a reality in my life. I had decided to work at an inner city Salvation Army Day Camp in Philadelphia for the summer after I graduated from college. So I lived in the damp basement of this inner city Salvation Army for a whole summer. One thing that I can remember doing when life got boring was turning on the lights at night and seeing how many cockroaches I could stomp on as they were scurrying back to the drains.

One day, I locked my keys in my car. I was visibly upset with myself as I was preparing to call a locksmith when one of the young men who was a regular at the gym noticed me. *What's the problem*, he asked? I told him. *Well, what kind of car do you have?* I have a 1963 Plymouth Sport Fury, I answered. *That's no sweat*, he replied. I remember walking with him out to the car, and in less time than it would have taken for me to reach into my pocket, pull out my keys and unlock the door (if I would have had my keys) that eleven year old had that door open. From that day on I have never put much confidence in locks. I use locks because they are certainly a deterrent, but I don't put all my faith in them.

Putting our trust in the Lord for protection does not mean that we will never be robbed. God allows some of his children to be robbed for some reason known only to him. God allowed David's home city to be sacked and looted while he and his men were away on a mission. But we won't be robbed unless God allows it to happen in his plan for our lives. This confidence can bring a peace of heart and mind that no amount of money and no security system can give.

David had experienced situations in life where his back was to the wall and he had to trust in the Lord. He had been in the back of a cave that Saul had chosen for his personal relief. His enemy had been just a few feet from him as he was trapped in the back of that cave with no way to escape. Saul had even decided to lie down and sleep for a while in the coolness of that cave. David had to suffer the prolonged agony of waiting, not knowing if he would be detected. David ended up sneaking up on the sleeping Saul and cutting off a corner of his robe.

But David learned an invaluable lesson at this time. In the final analysis, only God can protect our lives. God is the giver of life; God is the sustainer of life; and God is the protector of our lives. If we are walking in God's will down the pathway of life, we can have the confidence that no harm will befall us outside of the permissive will of God himself. That kind of assurance can bring peace to our hearts and minds.

Psalm 16:10 also has a tremendous prophetic significance:

Because you will not abandon me to the grave, nor will you let your Holy One see decay. (Psalm 16:10)

This statement, while certainly true of David, goes far beyond the scope of David's life, finding its ultimate fulfillment in the life of the Lord Jesus Christ. In fact, this verse was quoted in Peter's sermon on the day of Pentecost as referring to Christ. And what comfort this prophecy must have brought to our Savior as he was making that lonely journey to the cross as he realized that he could place his life in the hands of God the Father for protection. For while it was God's will to allow evildoers to take the physical life of his Messiah so that the ultimate payment for sin could be made, God would never allow the grave to hold him for he would protect his one and only Son from the decay of death.

God not only provided direction and protection for his servant David, but he also provided fellowship for him in this life with the promise of an eternal relationship to follow.

You have made known to me the path of life; you will fill me with joy in your presence, with eternal pleasures at your right hand. (Psalm 16:11)

What a testimony! *You have made known to me the path of life.* God had given his direction and counsel to David. God had anointed him to be king and had now put him into that position. *You will fill me with joy in your presence.* David had grown in his relationship with the Lord so that he had experienced fellowship with God, and this gave to him great confidence as he anticipated even greater fellowship with God yet in this life and in the life to come. *With eternal pleasures at your right hand.* David had the confidence that this life was just the beginning of an eternal relationship with God. And this gave to him great confidence and optimism as he looked towards the future.

The best path of life is God's path of life. While it is true that life can be confusing at times, God gives to his children counsel and direction so that they can know the course of his path of life and can walk it with confidence. While it is true that life can often be dangerous, God gives to his children protection so that they can walk his path of life with peace of heart. And while it is true that life can sometimes be lonely, God offers to his children his own presence and fellowship now. And he also gives to them the promise of an eternal life to follow.

Abebe Bicila was born in Ethiopia. His family was extremely poor so everyone in the family had to chip in just so the family could survive. Now what could Abebe do to help the family out? Well, he couldn't get a job because there were no jobs to get. But perhaps he could hunt and help secure food for the family. The problem was the fact that Abebe did not have a gun, or a sling-shot, or a blow-gun or any other means of hunting, and the family was too poor to secure a weapon. So Abebe used what he did have. He used his legs. Pheasants were one of the family's favorite foods. Abebe learned to run after pheasants.

Now many might be skeptical of Abebe's plan. Aren't Ethiopian pheasants smart enough to run away from a man trying to grab them? Of course they are, and the pheasants would scurry away from Abebe. But Abebe would continue running after them. He would keep running and running until the pheasants literally could no longer run from exhaustion. Then Abebe would pick up the exhausted bird and return with a meal for his family.

Someone heard of the tremendous endurance that Abebe Bicila had developed, and they told some governmental leaders. The leaders contacted Abebe and asked him if he would represent Ethiopia in the 1960 Olympic Games in Rome. Well, this was certainly an honor and Abebe would be pleased to do this. So Abebe Bicila joined the few other athletes from Ethiopia as they traveled to Rome for the Olympic Games. Hardly anyone noticed the Ethiopian team as they made their way to the Olympic Village for their small group was such an undistinguished one. And even fewer people noticed Abebe Bicila. Nobody had ever heard of him. And his appearance, well, let's just say that he looked just like the poor peasant that he was. In fact, when Abebe came out to sign in for the race, if anyone noticed him at all it was with a sense of shock and surprise. Abebe was not dressed in the modern marathon attire of lightweight shorts and featherweight shoes, but he rather looked just like the Ethiopian peasant that he was as he entered the race. But Abebe was entered under the flag of Ethiopia, and he joined the many other runners at the starting line.

The gun sounded, and the athletes sprinted ahead jockeying for position. No one paid any attention to Abebe for he was far back in the pack. But as the race continued, Abebe began to make his presence felt. With the endurance gained from chasing hundreds of pheasants, Abebe began to pass runner after runner. When the race was over, Abebe Bicila had not only won the gold medal in the marathon race, becoming the first black African to take home an Olympic gold medal, but he had also set a world's record time of two hours, fifteen minutes and fifteen seconds.

And perhaps as amazing as his endurance was the fact that he had run the entire race without the gear that would represent the latest in sport's technology - lightweight clothing and featherweight shoes. No, Abebe had run the entire race just as he would have chasing a pheasant. Now happily, Ethiopian dress is very lightweight, but it did mean that Abebe Bicila ran twenty-six miles and three hundred and eighty-five yards, the entire marathon against other world class runners, barefooted.

How many times does the world look past the Abebe Bicilas? How many times do people ignore those with great potential who do not appear from the outside to be that gifted? How many times do we personally fail to see potential in one another? How many times do we even look at ourselves as Abebe Bicilas, failing to realize the potential that God has created within us?

Experts agree that a person's self-esteem has a great influence on his or her achievements and quality of life. How we view ourselves has a direct impact upon how we view others and life in general. Yet this area of having a realistic and healthy self-esteem is one with which we all wrestle. For it is so easy to go to one of two extremes in considering our self-image.

Many people have a low self-esteem. They have little self-confidence; they don't feel that they are of much value; they feel that everyone around them is more capable and worthy than they. This is an unrealistic and crippling extreme for all of us have worth, value and greater potential than we will ever realize.

But there is another extreme that is just as dangerous to our wellbeing. Many think more highly of themselves than they should. Many feel superior to others around them. They have more confidence in themselves than is warranted. They feel that the world really should revolve around them. They become arrogant and egotistical. This is also an unrealistic and dangerous extreme for we all must accept ourselves for who we are in order to be contented in life.

A high school survey found that only two percent of high school students rated themselves below the fiftieth percentile in leadership ability. Twenty-five percent of the students actually claimed to be in the top one percent of their class in leadership ability. Now it doesn't take a genius to realize that these percentages just can't match reality. Fifty percent have to be below average; one out of four can't be in the top one percent.

One of the goals of our educational system has been to build a healthy self-esteem into students. It seems that they might be doing too good of a job in this area for in the very highly valued trait of leadership skills, most young people in this high school are thinking unrealistically.

One of David's greatest areas of strength was in his view of himself. David had a very realistic and healthy self-esteem. We can learn great lessons from him in this area. Psalm 8 reveals both David's personal self-esteem and his view of humans as a whole.

O LORD, our Lord, how majestic is your name in all the earth! You have set your glory above the heavens. From the lips of children and infants you have ordained praise because of your enemies, to silence the foe and the avenger. When I consider your heavens, the work of your fingers, the moon and the stars, which you have set in place, what is man that you are mindful of him, the son of man that you care for him? You made him a little lower than the heavenly beings and crowned him with glory and honor. You made him ruler over the works of your hands; you put everything under his feet: all flocks and herds, and the beasts of the field, the birds of the air, and the fish of the sea, all that swim the paths of the seas. O LORD, our Lord, how majestic is your name in all the earth! (Psalm 8:1-9)

There are **two major thoughts** that are bantered back and forth in this psalm. One is the **apparent insignificance of humans** and the other is our **true and real potential.** Our apparent insignificance is found in our natural view of ourselves. Our apparent insignificance is found in looking at ourselves through our own eyes. Our true and real potential is found in God's created purpose for each of us. Our true and real potential is found in looking at ourselves through God's eyes. In speaking of the human race in general, David also reveals his personal view of himself, of course, as a member of this human race.

David admits that we appear to be insignificant when compared to both heavenly bodies and heavenly beings. *When I consider the heavens, the work of your fingers, the moon and the stars, which you have set in place, what is man that you are mindful of him? You made him a little lower than the heavenly beings? (Psalm 8:3,4)*

The natural inclination of each of us as human beings is to compare ourselves with others outside of ourselves. Whenever we do this, we are normally led to think less of ourselves. How often do we compare ourselves with other people, people more gifted and capable than we? When we do this, we are led to think less of ourselves. David is doing this same thing with both heavenly bodies and heavenly beings here.

Humans are dwarfed by this earth on which we live. Many of us have seen natural wonders on vacation and have come away amazed at the wonder of God's creation on this earth. The delicate balance of nature in the forests surrounding us, the rugged beauty and enormous majesty of the mountains, the awesome and fearful power of the ocean waters all seem to dwarf us by their magnificence. Certainly, we can view ourselves as being insignificant compared to the immensity of the earth upon which we live.

But then when we consider the magnitude of other heavenly bodies we can feel even more infinitesimal. Our sun could contain over three hundred thousand earths. Its diameter is over a hundred times the diameter of the earth. The sun's diameter is greater than the distance between the earth and the moon. If we feel dwarfed by the magnitude of our earth, think of how we could feel when compared to the sun?

Then we go on to realize that the sun is not even among the greatest of the celestial bodies in the heavens. In fact, every single star that we can see at night with the naked eye is larger and greater than our sun. The star, Deneb, for instance is sixty thousand times brighter than our sun, but it is so far away from the earth that it appears much smaller. The light that we see today from Deneb left that star just after Jesus Christ lived on this earth, and it has been traveling from that time on at the speed of a hundred and eighty-six thousand miles per second to get to us now. Is it any wonder why the natural response of David was to write *when I consider the heavens, what is man?* Truly man seems to be insignificant.

But not only do the heavenly bodies dwarf us, but also the heavenly beings God has created make us appear to be so weak and helpless as well. The myriads of angelic beings that God has created, each one with the speed to be able to dart from location to location in fractions of a second, each one with strength thousands of times greater than ours, each one with an intellect making the most brilliant person in the human race seem like an infant child, each one with such awesome appearance that humans who have seen them have fallen on their faces before these angelic beings trying to worship them as God himself until they were ordered to stop. Even as great a man as Daniel who was fearless before lions fell down as dead before the appearance of Gabriel the angel.

When we consider the host of angelic creations about us, certainly the natural response is *what is man, this seemingly insignificant creature, who has been made lower than these other heavenly beings?* In fact, from all outward appearances, we are not that significant a creation. We are less mobile than the birds that God has made; we are less powerful than the lions of the field; we are less able to care for ourselves than almost any other creation of God.   Certainly there is no less helpless creature at birth than the human baby. What is man anyway? Why is he significant at all?

But when we are seeing ourselves in this light, we are looking at ourselves only through human eyes. We must move on to see ourselves through God's eyes in order to complete our perspective for God has designed the human race to be a manifestation of his own glory and majesty. The only way to see ourselves properly as a race and to see ourselves truthfully as individuals is to look through God's eyes. Happily, we are able to do this through God's revealed Word for the Bible is divine revelation of the human race.

G.K. Chesterton once wrote, *whatever else may be said of man, this one thing is clear: he is not what he is capable of being.* There is much truth in that statement. We all know that both the human race as a whole and each of us as individuals have not reached the potential that has been created in us. How can we be such a remarkable creation of God? Why is this one who is totally helpless at birth actually the most powerful of God's creatures?

Can humans, who are so small in comparison to the other humongous works of God, be more important than they? Can we, who tremble under the force of the natural elements around us, actually have the potential for being the dominator of them? *Yes*, David would say. In spite of our seeming insignificance, in reality, we have been created in the very image and likeness of God to be the pinnacle of all his creation. And the very areas of our seeming insignificance are those given by David as illustrations of our dignity and potential in the eyes of God.

Whereas it appears that humans are dwarfed by the magnitude of creation around us, in reality, in God's eyes, we have been created to exercise dominion over this earth. We have been created to have dominion over this earth today and we will rule over it one day. *You made him ruler over the works of your hands; you put everything under his feet: all flocks and herds, and the beasts of the field, the birds of the air, and the fish of the sea, all that swim the paths of the seas. (Psalm 8:6-8)*

Gordis once said, *a man should carry two stones in his pocket. On one should be inscribed, "I am but dust and ashes." On the other, "For my sake was the world created." And he should use each stone as he needs it.* It appears to be a paradox and in a sense it is. How could one who came from the earth, one who is made up of part of the earth and one whose physical body will return one day to the earth actually be the ruler over the earth? It seems impossible to us for to be created from the earth would imply subservience to it. And so those who have developed an evolutionary theory of development logically do make humans just part of the machine, part of the cycle, on the same level with all other animated life. And there are many who worship "mother earth" today.

But God says that he created the human race in his own image and likeness. (Genesis 1:26,27) This is what gives us our dignity. It is not the animated dust of this body, but rather the sculptor who formed that dust. Just as we don't honor the paints, but rather recognize that it is the name and ability of the artist that gives the ultimate value to a painting, so it must be realized that we have been created to be lords of the universe because that was the Lord's design for us. And we each have the potential created within us to exercise dominion over the rest of God's creation.

David also amazingly wrote that humans even have greater dignity than the heavenly beings. *You made him a little lower than heavenly beings* (this could be translated *you made him lower than heavenly beings for a little while), and crowned him with glory and honor. (Psalm 8:5)* There is a great prophetic statement that is found here. It certainly is true that the human race in its present sinful state is now lower in God's creative order than the angelic hosts who have never fallen into sin. But the indication is that this is just temporary.

Humans, and humans alone, have been created in the image and likeness of God himself with all of the dignity that is inherent with that position. History records that God sent his one and only Son to become human. Christ never became any other form of creation, but became a member of the human race alone. God has exalted humans above all of his other creation by personally identifying with us.

History records that Jesus Christ, the God-man, died upon the cross of Calvary to pay the penalty for the sins of the human race so that we can know forgiveness from sins. The Bible tells us that God's design is for us to become like Jesus Christ his only Son. (1 John 3:2)

One day, when we see the Lord Jesus Christ, we will become like him. And in that position, we will rule and reign with him over all of creation. This earth will be subdued under our rule during the millennial kingdom. Even angels will be recognized as being subservient to the redeemed for Paul reminded his readers that they would judge angels someday. (1 Corinthians 6:3)

At this time, at this very moment, if we are in the Lord Jesus Christ, God sees us in that position. As amazing as that might seem to us, as much as it contradicts our feelings of insignificance, God sees us as his children, co-heirs with Jesus Christ himself. (Romans 8:17) Even though he didn't have all the revelation that we have today, David saw this truth. He saw how the human race in its creation and purpose brought praise and majesty to God. So he fought off the temptation toward insignificance. David tempered his feelings with the clear revelation that God had given to him.

Now there are **two applications** of these truths that are critically important. First of all, in light of God's creation of the human race and in light of his attitude towards us, **people should treat one another with dignity and respect.** We have to realize that our attitudes and actions towards one another reflect directly on what we think of God. God has created us in his own image. Therefore, our actions toward our neighbor is seen by God as an action against himself. If we harm our fellow man, we are directing harm against God himself. That is the reason for God saying to Noah, *whoever sheds the blood of* man, by man shall his blood be shed, for in the image of God has God made man. (Genesis 9:6)

But on the other hand, if we help our neighbor, we are directing aid toward God himself. Jesus taught his disciples this principle in Matthew 25. He was speaking of a time of judgment when people would be rewarded for giving food, water, clothing and hospitality to God himself. They would naturally wonder when they had this privilege and so would ask, "Lord, when did we see you hungry and feed you, or thirsty and give you something to drink? When did we see you a stranger and invite you in, or needing clothes clothe you?" (Matthew 25:37,38)

Jesus gave God's rational in the next verses. The king will reply, "I tell you the truth, whatever you did for one of the least of these brothers of mine, you did for me." (Matthew 25:40) You see, actions performed for those created in God's image out of respect for their dignity are viewed by the Creator as actions performed to God himself. To handle the artist's canvas with care is to show respect to the painter.

A story is told by Leo Tolstoy, the prolific Russian author. One day he was walking down the street when he happened to pass a poor beggar who was asking for some help. Tolstoy searched through his pockets but couldn't even find one coin. Taking the beggar's hand in his own he apologized, don't be angry with me, brother, but I have no money in my pockets. The poor man's face brightened through the streaks of dirt that covered it and he replied, but you have given me more than I asked for - you called me "brother".

We might not have the means to solve all of the world's financial problems but we all do have it in our power to give respect to others. The follower of Jesus Christ recognizes that to honor a fellow human being with dignity and respect is to honor God himself.

But there is **another application** that also must be seen. There is only one way to reach our potential as human beings. Sin tries to devalue each of us. Sin brings with it all kinds of feelings of insignificance. Sin has marred that image God created in us so that it is almost beyond recognition. But God, who originally created us in his own image, has also made the provision so that this image might be restored in each of us. The second person of the Triune Godhead, the Lord Jesus Christ, became a human and thus exalted the human race above all the rest of creation. Jesus Christ provided the atonement for our sins so that we might be freed to reach our potential. But we will never reach that created potential unless we do so in Christ Jesus. If anyone tries to reach his potential solely on his own, he is doomed to failure because he is fighting against the Maker, the Creator. It is only as we accept Jesus Christ into our lives and dedicate ourselves to live for him that we can then begin to see ourselves through the eyes of God. We can try to pump up our images all we want with humanistic means, but the results will only be short-lived. And just like a balloon that has been blown up is released to shrivel back down again, we will shortly be overwhelmed with our seeming insignificance as we compare ourselves with the apparent greatness of all the creation around us. But as we become a member of God's own family, as we become more and more aware of all that God has done uniquely for us, as we realize all that we mean to God, as we grow in our character to actually become more and more like Jesus Christ and see these supernatural improvements within us, as we begin to see ourselves through the eyes of God himself, then we begin to realize our created dignity.

And a further amazing result begins to occur as well. As we begin to have a balanced, realistic view of ourselves, we begin to reveal God to others through our lives as well. This was Jesus' design for his disciples. The Lord Jesus Christ made the claim that he was God's light to this world. *I am the light of the world. Whoever follows me will never walk in darkness, but will have the light of life. (John 8:12)* It's not difficult for us to recognize this truth for God sent his Son into this world to reveal his truth to us. But then Jesus went a step further and commissioned his followers to be *light* as well.

In his famous Sermon on the Mount, Jesus instructed his disciples, y*ou are the light of the world . . . let your light shine before men, that they may see your good deeds and praise your Father in heaven. (Matthew 5:14,16)* Just as the moon has no light of its own but is a faithful reflector of the light of the sun throughout the night, so it is God's design for his children to reflect the light of the Lord Jesus Christ as they follow their Savior and allow his light to shine through their lives. Only then is it possible for human beings to reach the great potential that God has created for them. Only then will human beings have a proper, balanced self-esteem in life.

TRUSTING IN HORSES
Chapter 11

The air was filled with anticipation among music lovers in Mexico City on that warm night in 1975. Jose Serebrier had come to town. That gifted orchestral conductor from Uruguay was scheduled to direct a combined orchestral and choral concert that very evening. Music lovers had anticipated this concert for months. The hours of the day couldn't pass quickly enough for them.

Backstage, there was quite another conversation taking place. Close friends of Serebrier were trying to convince him to use a baton to conduct the concert that evening. Now Jose had never used a baton before. He was gifted in using his hands to convey all of his desires to his musicians. But Serebrier's close associates convinced him that these Mexican musicians would be more used to being led with a baton, that he would have greater control if he used one. Finally, Jose Serebrier relented. He would try a baton for the first time that evening.

The concert started well. The musicians in the orchestra were keen and alert, anticipating his every direction. The chorus was in good voice, singing enthusiastically. And then, suddenly, in the midst of the concert it happened. In a wild flurry trying to muster enthusiasm and crescendo, Jose Serebrier stabbed himself with his own baton. He drove the baton his right hand was holding completely through his left hand so that it actually came out the other side. In an instant the instruments and voices fell silent as blood gushed all over the podium. The concert came to an abrupt end as Jose was rushed off to the hospital.

Needless to say, that was the only performance where Jose Serebrier ever used a baton in his conducting. But in that one time, he distinguished himself. People who attended that concert probably would have forgotten the musical renditions by now. But they will never forget the conductor who once tried to lead with a baton and ended up stabbing himself with it.

It is important to practice with equipment before going public with it, isn't it? There is no feeling quite as helpless as trying to get used to some strange equipment in the heat of battle, when the pressure is on. No matter how gifted or proficient a person might be, he will not be at his best if he is using equipment that is strange to him. It's better to practice in private, to get used to the necessary equipment, before using it under the pressure of performance.

David knew the importance of this principle. He was a man who had a natural aptitude for military conflict. He was courageous in spirit. And he seemed to have a natural knack for outsmarting the opponent's plans. But David realized as well the necessity of being prepared for battle.

When King Saul tried to persuade David as a young teenager to use his armor to battle the giant named Goliath, David resisted the temptation. Humanly speaking, it would have been a great temptation to go into battle wearing the king's armor. It would have been seen as an honor to wear the King's personal armor. It would have been the best available protection. Saul had one of the few swords found in Israeli hands. But the armor didn't fit David. Saul was head and shoulders taller than David. And David had not practiced sufficiently with Saul's armor to be confident in its use. So when David went out to face Goliath, after placing his faith and trust solidly in the Lord, he took with him only his proven sling with five smooth stones. David had a plan and he executed that plan to perfection in slaying that great Philistine champion.

David continued this pattern throughout his life in his military conquests. He always had a pattern, a strategy that he carried out. This pattern was comfortable for him; it was one that he had proven to be true. As his leadership abilities, army and available weaponry grew, David was able to take on progressively larger challenges. But he never forgot or strayed from his commitment to trust first and foremost in the Lord. Just as he had expressed his faith in the Lord for victory before that battle with Goliath as a teenager, so David continued that pattern of battle throughout his life.

Psalm 20 is called *a liturgy for preparation for battle* by Biblical scholars. It reveals to us from David's own viewpoint how he prepared himself as king to defend his country against the enemies that surrounded it. And make no mistake about it, from a practical standpoint, this function of the royal throne was among the most important. For a king in these days was evaluated by the strength of his nation and his ability to defend his country against enemy threats.

Most kings began their preparation for battle in the council room with their advisors and generals suggesting plans. David began his preparation for battle by seeking God's face in his sanctuary.

May the LORD answer you when you are in distress; may the name of the God of Jacob protect you. May he send you help from the sanctuary and grant you support from Zion. May he remember all your sacrifices and accept your burnt offerings. (Psalm 20:1-3)

It was only after David had sacrificed to the Lord and sought his help and direction in God's sanctuary that he would then sit down and draw up his battle plans.

May he give you the desire of your heart and make all your plans succeed. (Psalm 20:4)

Many Bible scholars agree that, in the context, the plans that are spoken of here are battle plans, military strategy to gain an advantage over the enemy.

David would then go before the Lord in prayer, seeking God's face until he had the assurance that he was in God's perfect timing. He then could enter the battle with the confidence that victory had been secured.

We will shout for joy when you are victorious and will lift up our banners in the name of our God. May the LORD grant all your requests. Now I know that the LORD saves his anointed; he answers him from his holy heaven with the saving power of his right hand. (Psalm 20:5,6)

It is interesting that the verb translated *saves* is in the Hebrew prophetic perfect tense. It looks at a future event as already having been completed. Having sought God's direction in his sanctuary, David laid out the best battle plans conceivable to him, and then he prayed through those plans until he had the confidence that they represented exactly what God wanted him to do. So when David entered a battle, he engaged in the conflict with the absolute assurance that the victory had already been secured. It's no wonder that there isn't a battle recorded in either Biblical or extra-Biblical records where David was defeated. For David had found a sure fire pattern for military victory.

David recognized that there were two ways to enter a battle with an enemy, and he summarized these **two philosophies of conflict** in verse 7. His insights are applicable for each of us even to this very day. For we all face battles in life. They might not be physical battles fought out in a grassy valley with swords and spears, but they are battles nonetheless.

Now how we plan for these battles and how we engage in these battles are most important, for our preparation and methodology used in battle will probably determine whether we are victorious or not. David indicates that there are basically two ways to wage the battles of life. He revealed these two ways in a succinct manner in verse 7.

Some trust in chariots and some in horses, but we trust in the name of the LORD our God. (Psalm 20:7)

The first way to fight a battle is **to trust in chariots or horses.** Now at first glance, we have a tendency to think David's words to be outdated. Most of us don't even own a chariot or a horse. And even if we do own one, nobody would be tempted to trust in them for victory in a significant battle today. But David's words, while certainly appropriate for his day in a literal sense, can also be taken symbolically signifying a trusting in the flesh, a trusting in our own human-made plans and powers.

Most kings in David's day would stockpile weapons. They would accumulate as many swords, spears and arrows as they could. And when they thought they had sufficient power to dominant a neighboring kingdom, they would make their move. Among the most powerful of the weapons in David's day were chariots and horses for one man in a chariot could mow down hundreds of men on foot; and one man on horseback could move around faster than hundreds of men on foot. So the army with the most chariots and horses had a strategic military advantage. It would be like the army with the most fighter jets and missiles today. A smaller army with air superiority can defeat a much larger army with just land equipment in our day.

Now David certainly didn't discount weaponry. He carefully trained his men and secured as many weapons as he could. But David didn't put the bulk of his trust in the military hardware that he had. Frankly, if David would have relied solely upon his military equipment, he would have lost every single battle in his early life. He would have been defeated by Goliath who had superior weapons to his. He would have been killed by Saul who had more manpower than he had. He would have lost all of these early battles against the Philistines who had all of the chariots and horses. David, from all human measures, didn't stand a chance in any of these battles. But he won every one of them. The reason for his victory is that he didn't put his trust in chariots and horses.

The natural tendency that we all have when going into battle is to put our faith in chariots and horses. What are some of the chariots and horses that we trust in today? We often put our trust in our minds and intellect. Knowledge is generally recognized as power today. Many times we feel that we must have the latest equipment, the technological edge to win the battles of life. Money is also trusted today. How many times do we hear the phrase *money is power?* It is the person or organization with the financial resources that has a big edge in winning the battle today in the minds of most people.

There are many others who use manipulation to their advantage. Getting control of the situation is what they seek. Sales people are taught how to control the conversation. Business executives go to seminars to learn how to control meetings. Family members learn how to manipulate each other to get their way. The key is securing power and leverage. Business partners often have secret meetings to make sure that they have the majority of votes before they go into the conference room. Family members often try to get others on their side in the conflict. These all are examples of trusting in chariots and horses today. These are examples of relying upon our natural human abilities and values.

Now it is interesting that most of these values are good (or at least can be beneficial) if used properly. Education is certainly a good thing. A person is wise to value the development of the mind and intellectual capacities. Technology certainly can be a good thing. Technology has enhanced the quality of all of our lives. Money is a good thing. It certainly is better to have some resources than to be destitute. Power is a good thing if used wisely. Meeting together and discussing issues to get a consensus can be a good thing. Many needless conflicts could be avoided with a productive meeting where a win/win solution is worked out. But if we are trusting in these alone for victory in the battles of life, we are going to be disappointed.

In the year 1923, a yearly review of a major magazine listed the five most successful and powerful men in our country. These men were Schwab (the President of the largest Steel Company in our nation), Howard Hopsen (the President of the largest Gas Company in our nation), Richard Whitney (the President of the New York Stock Exchange), Arthur Cooper (the key influence in the Chicago stock exchange that basically controlled the prices of our agricultural products) and Mr. C. Rivermore (who was called the *Great Bear of Wall Street*). These were the men who controlled our country the magazine claimed. These were the men who had it all - money, power, fame, and prestige. These were the men who had climbed to the top of the ladders in their perspective fields and had won the battles of life.

But do you know what happened shortly after to each of these five who were touted as the most influential men in our nation by this major magazine? Schwab died a pauper; Howard Hopsen lived out his life in a psychiatric facility; Richard Whitney was released from prison near the end of his life so that he could die at home; Arthur Cooper died in a foreign country, penniless; and Rivermore committed suicide. All of these men had trusted in chariots and horses but their weaponry and philosophy of battle ultimately failed them in life.

David exemplifies a better way to fight the battles of life. David made **trusting in the name of the Lord** his top priority in life.

Some trust in chariots and some in horses, but we trust in the name of the LORD our God. They are brought to their knees and fall, but we rise up and stand firm. (Psalm 20:7,8)

David discovered the secret to winning the battles of life and he outlined that battle plan in four steps that he took.

First, **David sought direction from the Lord** in his sanctuary. David would bring his sacrifice before the Lord and ask God to give him direction for how the battle should be waged. David speaks of this step in the first three verses.

May the LORD answer you when you are in distress; may the name of the God of Jacob protect you. May he send you help from the sanctuary and grant you support from Zion. May he remember all your sacrifices   and accept your burnt offerings. (Psalm 20:1-3)

Then David **would make his plan carefully** based upon the direction that he had received from the Lord. He talked about this in the fourth verse

May he give you the desire of your heart and make all your plans succeed. (Psalm 20:4)

David's third step would be **to pray through the plan** until he had the assurance from God that it was his divine will, that it would be successful, and that it was the right time to execute the plan. David speaks of this step in verses 5,6.

We will shout for joy when you are victorious and will lift up our banners in the name of our God. May the LORD grant all your requests.   Now I know that the LORD saves his anointed; he answers him from his holy heaven with the saving power of his right hand. (Psalm 20:5,6)

Only after these other steps were taken would David step out **to execute the plan**, confident that victory had already been secured.

A very clear illustration of how David carried out his battle plan is found in the twenty-third chapter of 1 Samuel. This chapter pictures David in a situation where he was hopelessly out-numbered. The Philistines had just captured the town of Keilah. David, at this time, had just started running from King Saul. He had a few men with him, but not very many. But David did have Abiathar, the High Priest, who had escaped from the Levite city of Nob with the ephod. The first six verses of the chapter outline David's situation clearly.

When David was told, "Look, the Philistines are fighting against Keilah and are looting the threshing floors," he inquired of the LORD, saying, "Shall I go and attack these Philistines?"

The LORD answered him, "Go, attack the Philistines and save Keilah."

But David's men said to him, "Here in Judah we are afraid. How much more, then, if we go to Keilah against the Philistine forces!"

Once again David inquired of the LORD, and the LORD answered him, "Go down to Keilah, for I am going to give the Philistines into your hand."

So David and his men went to Keilah, fought the Philistines and carried off their livestock. He inflicted heavy losses on the Philistines and saved the people of Keilah. (Now Abiathar son of Ahimelech had brought the ephod down with him when he fled to David at Keilah.)   (1 Samuel 23:1-6)

When David heard that the Philistines had attacked Keilah, the Bible says that he inquired of the Lord as to whether or not he should go up against them to deliver his fellow Israelites. Abiathar the High Priest inquired of God and gave to David the divine direction that he desired. *Go and attack the Philistines and save Keilah.* When David shared this direction with his men, they questioned the wisdom of the strategy. *We could never take this city from the Philistines,* they protested. *They have too much manpower, too many chariots, too many horses.*

So the Bible says that David actually inquired of the Lord a second time to be sure, and God gave the same direction to him again. Having received this clear direction from God, David carefully laid out plans as to how to recapture the city. Then, assured of God's direction and timing, David surprised the Philistines in an attack, inflicting heavy losses on them and capturing back the city of Keilah for his fellow countrymen (1 Samuel 23:5).

He had been underpowered and undermanned. There was no earthly hope for him to have been victorious in this venture. He was just a vagabond fugitive with a few other refugees with him. And he was fighting against the most powerful military machine in the Middle East. Even his own men were not supportive of the plan. But David had learned at an early age not to trust in chariots and horses, but to trust in the name of the Lord his God. He knew that God was more powerful than any earthly kingdom. So if he followed God's direction in life, he knew he would be successful.

One of the hardest lessons to learn in this life is that the battles we fight are not ultimately physical battles. It doesn't matter whether we are in a struggle at work or in a conflict within our family or in an inner battle that we are waging in our own lives or something that is happening at church. Behind all physical appearances, there are spiritual forces at work. This is the arena where the real battles of life are waged. If our battles are to be won, they must ultimately be won on this level.

The Apostle Paul wrote some insightful words found in 2 Corinthians 10.

For though we live in this world, we do not wage war as the world does. The weapons we fight with are not the weapons of the world. On the contrary, they have divine power to demolish strongholds. We demolish arguments and every pretension that sets itself up against the knowledge of God, and we take captive every thought to make it obedient to Christ. (2 Corinthians 10:3-5)

The Apostle Paul looked at the battles of life in the same way that David did. Even though he lived a thousand years after David had died, Paul understood the necessity of engaging in the battles of life with spiritual weaponry. He concluded his letter to the church at Ephesus by outlining various pieces of armor that God has provided for his children. It shouldn't surprise anyone that Paul, like David, was also successful in the battles of life. We also must be spiritually equipped if we are to wage our life battles successfully.

Some trust in chariots and some in horses, but we trust in the name of the Lord our God. They will be brought to their knees and fall, but we will rise up and stand firm. (Psalm 20:7,8))

Marcus didn't need it. It was foolish for him to buy it. But Marcus wanted it. He desperately wanted to own it. So Marcus showed up with many others on that day of the auction.

The bidding started at ten thousand, certainly a bargain in anyone's eyes. But then it quickly escalated to move up the ladder. Fifteen thousand; eighteen thousand; twenty thousand. Now the bidding slowed. They were moving out of the range of most of the bidders. Marcus looked over into the eyes of his only remaining competitor, a man named Flavius. Marcus could see that his rival wanted to own it as much as he did. But Marcus knew that he had the edge. He knew that he had more money. He would just keep raising the ante until he outbid his competitor. Twenty-one thousand; twenty-two thousand; twenty-three thousand. The response was slowing now. Twenty-four thousand; twenty-five thousand. Finally, Flavius was silent. And when that gavel hit the podium and he heard the auctioneer shout *sold,* Marcus knew that his lifelong dream had now come true. He finally owned that which he had always dreamed that he might one day possess.

It is ironic that the item that Marcus sacrificed so much for would soon cost him his life. For Marcus would only live with his prized possession for two months. Then it would kill him. Marcus wasn't involved in an auction that occurred this year or even this century. No, this auction was almost two millennia ago, in March of the year 193 after Christ was born.   And the twenty-five thousand that Marcus paid for the object of his dreams was not in dollars, but it was rather in a currency called sesterces.   You see the elite Roman Praetorian guard had mutinied.   They had grabbed control of the Roman Empire. Then they had devised a plan of how to get rich.

They would hold an auction. They would appeal to the covetous natures of Rome's richest patrons.   They would sell the entire Empire on the auction block and split up the money amongst them. Marcus Didius Julianus, one of Rome's most wealthy citizens, had swallowed the bait. Now he could say that he owned the Mighty Roman Empire. He was the Emperor of Rome. Two months later, Marcus was dead - assassinated.   He had given almost everything he had to own what he most desired. And now what he thought he owned had killed him.

Many people fall into the trap that took the life of Marcus Julianus. For it is part of our basic human natures to desire to own, to possess, to control. People will do almost anything to own something else. They will work day and night; they will take all kinds of personal risks; they will leverage themselves to the limit. And too often, what they sacrifice so much to own ends up killing them. No, it doesn't assassinate them. It usually doesn't even kill them quickly.   But slowly, through stress, through anxieties, through all kinds of pressures, that which a person thinks he owns often ends up sapping the very life blood out of him.

One of the most important lessons that any person can learn in life is the one modeled by King David in Psalm 24. David was the king of the most powerful nation in the Middle East by the time he wrote these words. He had sacrificed and risked a great deal to get where he was. He could have been puffed up in pride over all of his accomplishments. He could have become enamored with all that he owned and controlled. He could have been obsessed with all kinds of anxieties and worries.

But instead of falling into these perilous traps, David exemplifies a realistic view of himself, God and his relationship towards material things. This allowed David to have a relationship with God in worship that was unparalleled in his day. It was David's relationship with God that allowed him to have joy, peace and contentment in his life.

The earth is the LORD's, and everything in it, the world, and all who live in it; for he founded it upon the seas and established it upon the waters.

Who may ascend the hill of the LORD? Who may stand in his holy place? He who has clean hands and a pure heart, who does not lift up his soul to an idol or swear by what is false. He will receive blessing from the LORD and vindication from God his Savior. Such is the generation of those who seek him, who seek your face, O God of Jacob.

Lift up your heads, O you gates; be lifted up, you ancient doors, that the King of glory may come in. Who is

*this King of glory? The LORD strong and mighty, the LORD
mighty in battle.*

*Lift up your heads, O you gates; lift them up, you
ancient doors, that the King of glory may come in. Who is
he, this King of glory? The LORD Almighty -- he is the King
of glory. (Psalm 24:1-10)*

David lays a solid foundation for worship in the first
two verses of this psalm. The history of this universe is
found in the struggle for ownership. By the time God
created the heavens and the earth, Lucifer had already
rebelled against God and had been cast out of heaven.
Many other angelic beings had followed him in this mutiny
against God. So when God created the beautiful garden of
Eden here on the earth and threw the sun and stars into
their heavenly orbits, the first thing that Satan did was to
try to grab ownership of the earth from God. He
commandeered the slithering body of a serpent and
tempted Eve to transgress God's commandments. Then
he used Eve to tempt Adam into willfully sinning against
God. He quickly had a foothold in their lives and through
their sinful rebellion, he tried to wrest the ownership of
this earth from God himself. He has been so successful
that the Bible even calls him the *Prince of the Power of the
Air* and *the God of this Age.*

The human race, in its sinful rebellion against God,
has also tried to claim ownership of this God-created
earth. It is interesting to note Cain's response to God's
punishment after he killed his brother, Abel, in a
premeditated manner. God, of course, was not pleased

with Cain's selfish and cruel action. So God punished Cain by exiling him to the outermost regions of the earth. *You will be a restless wanderer on the earth,* God ordered Cain as recorded in Genesis 4:12. But what did Cain do? He disobeyed God again. The first thing he did was to go to the land east of Eden and build a city in which to settle. He named this first city on planet earth *Enoch* after his firstborn son. It was as if Cain was trying to take ownership of the earth from God.

Now there is nothing inherently wrong with having the title to a piece of land or a house. God allowed his people to own property in the Bible. And we should be careful that we have proper title when we own a house so that our investment can be protected. But one of the differences between the godly and the ungodly in the Bible is found in their recognition of who ultimately is the owner of the earth and all that is contained within it. Godly people have always recognized that God is the ultimate creator and owner of everything.

Godly people have always realized that they have only been allowed a portion of the earth for their own usage because of God's gracious goodness to them. Ungodly people have devised every way imaginable from denying God's existence to creating clever theories like evolution in their attempts to take rightful ownership of this earth from God.

David's words are interesting here, especially in light of the fact that he had just systematically conquered all of the nations of the Middle East. In his day, that made him the recognized owner of these lands. In his day, David could have claimed the title *Lord of the Middle East* and nobody would have objected. But David recognized who the rightful owner of the earth was. The earth and all it contains belongs to the Lord. *The earth is the Lord's and everything in it,* David wrote.

This recognition is the foundation for true worship. When we come to worship God, we are honoring the owner of this planet and all that is in it. That means we are confessing that our own lives and all that we have earthly title to ultimately belong to the Lord. So he is the ultimate master; he is the ultimate title holder; he is the ultimate source and sustainer of all things. He alone deserves the recognition for that position, and we give him that recognition when we worship.

The next two verses reveal **qualifications for worship** that David acknowledged. For if we are to truly worship as great a being as God, it is only reasonable that we must come to him on his terms, not on ours. One of the tell-tale signs that we are trying to subtly wrestle ownership from God is found in our attempts to dictate the terms of our worship to God. Many people sadly try to worship God on their own terms. They will worship as long as it makes them feel good, or as long as God meets their needs, or as long as their style of music is played. Now, as we are going to see momentarily, God has graciously given to us many blessings as a result of our worship. But ultimately God must dictate the conditions of worship to us. We cannot dictate the conditions of our worship to God. That would be usurping his rightful position. David recognized this fact.

Who may ascend the hill of the LORD? Who may stand in his holy place? He who has clean hands and a pure heart, who does not lift up his soul to an idol or swear by what is false. (Psalm 24:3,4)

There are **three qualifications** that David sets forth here for one who is to be able to worship God as he should, namely purity, obedience and honesty.

The necessity for **purity** is found in the words *clean hands and a pure heart.* The hands are symbolic of our actions before the Lord. With the hands we do. Our activities in life must be consistent with God's standards if we are to ascend into his hill in worship for fellowship with him. The heart represents our affections. With the heart we desire, we love, we feel. If we are to ascend onto his hill in worship, we must do so with the proper love for the Lord. We must not be motivated by selfish, ulterior motives, but by the purity of a desire to know our Creator in a fuller way, with gratitude for who he is and all that he has done for us. We may not come to God with a hypocritical spirit, living one way but claiming to believe another. We must rather come in purity, with clean hands and a pure heart.

Now happily God does not put the burden of cleaning up our lives solely upon our shoulders before coming before him in worship. That would set an impossible task before us. Before the temple of the Lord, God placed the great bronze altar of sacrifice. So the worshipper would offer his sacrifice accepting God's cleansing for his sins before entering into worship with God. We recognize that Jesus Christ has provided the final sacrifice for sins today. But we must appropriate that sacrifice to our lives in order to have clean hands and a pure heart if we are to have any effective worship of God.

The necessity for **obedience** is found in the words *one who does not lift up his soul to an idol.* The first of the commandments that God gave to the children of Israel was to not make any graven image or idol representation of him. So this statement of David, being the first of God's commandments, probably represents not only itself but all of the commandments of God. Certainly we cannot hope to worship God if we do so while approaching idols, for that would be coming to God on our terms, not his.

But we must also be careful that, to the best of our knowledge, we are in obedience to all of God's commandments to us if we are to have effective worship of God. If we are in willful violation of God's commandments we will not be able to have the fellowship with God that will bring satisfying worship. In Psalm 66, the Psalmist wrote, *if I regard iniquity in my heart, the Lord will not hear me.*

The necessity for **honesty** is found in the words *one who does not swear by what is false.* God is a God of truth. We must come to him honestly. He cannot fellowship with that which is deceitful or false.

Now these are God's terms for worship that are based upon his unchanging character. God is a God of absolute purity; he is a righteous and holy God. God is infinite in all of His being; he cannot be contained in an idol or graven image. God is a God of truth; he is faithful in all of his promises. Therefore, our worship of him must be in purity, in obedience and in honesty.

The next couplet of verses allows us to see the wonderful results of worship.

He will receive blessing from the LORD and vindication from God his Savior. Such is the generation of those who seek him, who seek your face, O God of Jacob. (Psalm 24:5,6)

There are **two results of worship** that David enumerates here, namely blessing and vindication.

The word that is usually translated ***blessing*** in the Bible can also mean *prosperity, praise, gifts* or even a *treaty of peace.* The one who worships God on his terms is made prosperous by God. His soul and spirit is enriched. He is filled with joy and peace. God gives to him all kinds of treasures that no amount of money can ever purchase. It is amazing that God praises the one who worships him on his terms. The worshipper has come for the purpose of praising God.

But God, who will be a debtor to no person, ends up praising him. He lifts him up and exalts him. He honors him. David never lost the wonder of God exalting him from the lowly position of shepherding to the exalted position of being king of Israel. The one who worships God on God's terms receives gifts from God.

It is one of the ironies of worship that as we recognize God's rightful position as the owner of the earth and all that it contains, releasing our own selfish claims,

God is then free to give us all kinds of gifts and blessings. He delights in showering his goodness on his children. The one who worships God on God's terms receives a treaty of peace from God. He is at peace with his Creator. He has peace in his heart. He doesn't have to live his life in a state of enmity or warfare.

The word that is translated **vindication** in this Psalm is normally translated *righteousness* in the Bible. It can also mean *justice* or even *salvation*. The one who worships God on God's terms not only sees the righteousness of Almighty God but he also experiences growth in his own personal righteousness as well. He is put into a relationship with God whereby God can vindicate him, giving him righteousness and salvation.

It is important to remember that in David's day it was commonly recognized that while the subject kingdom was expected to pay tribute and give allegiance to the conquering kingdom, the conquering kingdom was expected to protect and save the subject kingdom when in danger. It is interesting that David seems to acknowledge this practice that was common knowledge in his day as he says that as the worshipper of God recognizes God's rightful position in his or her life, God then rewards the worshipper with vindication, justice and salvation. The worshiper is put into a position where he is protected by Almighty God himself.

David's conclusion to this Psalm reminds us of the contrasting attitude of another Old Testament king who also built a great empire. His name was Nebuchadnezzar; he built the mighty Babylonian Empire There were many similarities between David and Nebuchadnezzar. Both were obviously capable and courageous men. Both took nations that were disorganized politically and militarily and built them into great empires controlling the nations surrounding them. But there was also a great difference in the attitudes of these two men. Daniel describes Nebuchadnezzar standing on the roof of his palace overlooking the great city of Babylon and boasting of his accomplishments.

Is not this the great Babylon I have built as the royal residence, by my mighty power, and for the glory of my majesty? (Daniel 4:30)

Nebuchadnezzar's own confession revealed who he thought to be the King of glory? God had to humble this Babylonian king because he did not recognize who was the rightful owner of the earth and all that was in it. So the end of chapter four of Daniel describes a seven year period in Nebuchadnezzar's life when he lost his mind and wandered around the fields grazing like a cow.

But in Psalm 24 we have another great empire builder. David took a nation that was under the dominion and control of the Philistines and brought it to a position of dominance over the entire Middle East. But his attitude was completely different from Nebuchadnezzar's. When David asks the question, *who is this King of glory?*, his answer is *the Lord strong and mighty, the Lord mighty in battle, he is the King of glory.* David recognized who God was and gave to him the honor and glory due to His name.

And isn't it interesting that while most people have forgotten all about the accomplishments of Nebuchadnezzar, the King of Babylon, today, David is still honored by many across the world. How many boys bear the name Nebuchadnezzar? But David still remains a very popular name throughout much of the world. In fact, God would choose to have his one and only Son who came into this world to be given the title *the Son of David.*

God alone is the owner of the earth and all that is in it. He alone deserves worship and honor for who he is. When we worship God, we must come to him on his terms, not on ours. But nobody who sincerely worships God is ever disappointed, for the worshipper of God receives far more than he ever gives. That is just how great God is!

Todd was plagued by guilt. He felt so strongly that he had let his country down that he was ashamed to even show his face in public. Why would a man with such great potential and training feel so guilty? Why would a man who had been a prominent attorney, a respected statesman, the Secretary of War under two separate presidential administrations and Ambassador to Great Britain under yet another president feel that he had failed his country so much? Well, it was because of his tardiness. You see, Todd had trouble getting to appointments on time. And if you think that Todd was overreacting to a minor character flaw, consider these three situations of tardiness in Todd's life. At the age of thirty-eight, when Todd was Secretary of War under James Garfield, he was to meet the President at the train station. Todd got tied up in traffic and was late. Moments before Todd arrived at the station, President Garfield was shot and killed by an assassin's bullet. Twenty years later, when Todd was fifty-eight, in September of 1901, Todd had an appointment to meet President McKinley at the Pan American Exposition in Buffalo, NY. Again, Todd was late. When he arrived, he discovered that President McKinley had been shot. This wound also proved to be fatal to the President. So Todd spent the remainder of his life plagued by guilt, in seclusion, thinking that he had let his country down, vowing that he would never again be in the presence of another president.

But I failed to mention that third scene, didn't I? That scene happened some twenty years before President Garfield's assassination. Todd had been invited to join President and Mrs. Abraham Lincoln in their private box at the Ford Theater. Todd was late for the play. He arrived just in time to see them carrying President Lincoln's body out of the theater. If Todd had only been there on time, he reasoned, he would have been seated in the back of that box. Perhaps he would have been able to obscure the aim of Booth's bullet. So on three separate occasions, Todd had been late to an appointment with a United States president, and each time, the president had been assassinated. After the third time, Todd vowed that he would never see another president face to face. Everyone knew the guilt with which Todd lived because he loved his country so much and felt that he had failed it. But it was also because of his love for his family.

For of all those situations, the one that happened first, the one that took place in Ford's Theater, was the most difficult for Todd. For he always felt in his heart that, if he had been there on time, he could have been positioned to block the assassin's bullet. Instead, on that fateful night, Todd Lincoln not only lost his president, he also lost his father.

Guilt. There is nothing that has the potential to make life more miserable than guilt. Guilt can be relentless. Guilt can crush a person's spirit. Guilt can even produce physical symptoms in one's life. Guilt can negate even the greatest potential in life.

166

People try to cope with guilt in many differing ways. Some try to run from it. Others try to ignore it, hoping that it will somehow go away. Still others try to deny it, trying to convince themselves that it is only a figment of their imaginations. But in the final analysis, there is only one way to be free from the imprisoning power of guilt. Guilt must be faced head on. The source of the guilt must be examined. Then that source must be dealt with or removed. Only then can a person be freed from guilt in life.

If the feelings of guilt stem from a non-moral source, they must be rejected as an attempt of the enemy to hinder our spiritual growth. Failure to meet our own expectations or the expectations of others can produce a false guilt in our lives. The captain of the basketball team who fails to hit the jump shot at the buzzer to win the game for his team might experience strong feelings of guilt, thinking that he let down his team. But his missing a shot was not a moral issue. He just had placed too high of expectations on himself. Nobody can be expected to make every shot. He tried his best. He missed the shot. He must accept his own limitations and reject false guilt.

But when the feelings of guilt come from a moral failure, this sin must be dealt with in our lives if we are to be freed from the weight of guilt that can so easily destroy us and the potential that God has given to us.

We now enter a consideration of the darkest period morally in the life of King David. We have already looked at some psalms that reflect David's childhood. We have seen many psalms documenting that difficult period in his life when he was running from Saul, when God was preparing him for his rule. Then in the past several chapters, we have been looking at some psalms written after David had become King and built his empire into a powerful force in the Middle East.

We now enter yet another period of David's life. From all outward appearances, life couldn't have been better. David's kingdom was at its peak. All of the surrounding nations had been subdued under his power and were now paying tribute to him, giving him not only great influence but also lucrative wealth as well. But it was at this point that David would have his greatest moral failure.

It all started with David resting at ease in his palace while Joab, the commander in chief of his army, was out with the troops making sure that the empire was in order. It was the custom for the armies to periodically make the rounds collecting tribute and making sure that everything in the empire was going smoothly. David, from the vantage point of his lofty palace roof, saw the beautiful Bathsheba bathing on the roof of her house. He lusted after her and finally sent some of his servants to bring her to the palace so that he could commit adultery with her. After finding out that she was pregnant following their adulterous affair, David sent for her husband, Uriah, who was serving under Joab in the army. David instructed Joab to send Uriah under the pretext of receiving a report from him concerning the welfare of the army. David's plan, of course, was for Uriah to spend time with his wife after his long absence so that everyone would then think that

Bathsheba's baby was his. Uriah, however, thwarted the King's plans. A man of great character and integrity, Uriah refused to go and stay at his own home while his fellow soldiers were inconvenienced, sleeping in their tents. So because David was not able to get Uriah and his wife together even after a second try, he moved to plan B. David gave Uriah a sealed letter to deliver to Joab telling the commander-in-chief to place Uriah in the front of the battle line while an attack of a city wall was engaged. In the heat of the battle, Joab was to draw back the troops, leaving Uriah exposed to the enemy, effectively putting him to death. Joab knew nothing of what had been happening back in Jerusalem, of course, and obeyed the king's command thinking that there must be some good reason for David's order. Uriah was killed in battle. David then took the widow, Bathsheba, into his own household as one of his wives, and the cover-up was complete. An understanding of the cultural setting is important in order to realize the significance of David's plan here for if something like this scenario were to happen today, people would be very suspicious. But in David's day, he would have been highly regarded for such a response. There were no social security programs in ancient Israel. And there were few vocational opportunities for widows to support themselves. When David took Bathsheba into his own household, committing himself to provide for her needs for the rest of her life, this would have been viewed by the people as being an extremely generous gesture by the King to a war hero's family. So, in essence, David had committed both adultery and murder in secret and had come out looking like a kind and generous benefactor in public. It seemed to be the perfect cover-up. The only factors that David overlooked were the omniscient nature of God who sees and knows all things and his own guilty conscience having to live with his wicked actions. For while the sin of adultery might be considered a sin due to the weakness of his fleshly desires, the death of Uriah could be considered nothing short of premeditated, cold-blooded murder. David's guilty conscience was making his life miserable. He couldn't sleep at night; he was having trouble concentrating on his work during the day; there was no joy in his life anymore; he was just plain miserable all of the time. And this depressed lifestyle went on for about a year in David's life.

Finally, God sent his prophet, Nathan, to confront David concerning his sin. Nathan led David through the process of confession and restoration of fellowship with God so that the King could be freed from the prison of his own guilt. Now David would still have to suffer some consequences for his sins since our actions always bear consequences. But the heavy weight of the guilt was finally lifted from David's shoulders. David wrote two Psalms in response to this dark night of the soul in his life. Most Bible scholars feel that Psalm 51 was written shortly after Nathan's confrontation of David, and that Psalm 32 was written some time later after the King had been able to evaluate this event more. We will look at Psalm 51 in this chapter and Psalm 32 in the next one.

Psalm 51 reveals **six steps** that David took in this process of spiritual restoration. Now it is quite likely that

Nathan the Prophet helped David through this spiritually difficult time in his life. But David saw the necessity of these six steps in restoring his relationship with God that had been so damaged.

Step #1 - Confession of Sin:

Have mercy on me, O God, according to your unfailing love; according to your great compassion blot out my transgressions. Wash away all my iniquity and cleanse me from my sin. For I know my transgressions, and my sin is always before me. Against you, you only, have I sinned and done what is evil in your sight, so that you are proved right when you speak and justified when you judge. Surely I was sinful at birth, sinful from the time my mother conceived me. Surely you desire truth in the inner parts; you teach me wisdom in the inmost place. (Psalm 51:1-6)

There are two very difficult verses to interpret in this Psalm. The first one is verse 4. When David writes to God *against you only have I sinned*, we are tempted to object. What about Bathsheba? Didn't you defile her purity? What about Uriah? Didn't you sin against him in taking his life? What about your family who were all affected by your sin? And what about the nation? Didn't you betray the trust of your subjects in you as their king? How can you say that you only sinned against God here?

Certainly it is true that many people were affected by David's sin. But as this verse is considered in its context, David shows an insight into what the heart of his sin really was. While it is certainly possible to violate the rights of others, we can only break the holy and righteous standards of God. For other human beings do not have perfectly holy and righteous standards to break. Frankly, in the eyes of the world and the culture of David's day, this King of Israel had not done anything that neighboring kings would consider to be wrong. Kings often took beautiful women into their harems in this day. And if their husbands stood in the way, the king had the power to dispose of them. This was Abraham's fear as he journeyed both down into Egypt and also into the land of the Philistines with his wife, Sarah. In the eyes of the world, David had just exercised one of his prerogatives as king. But David here shows that he understood what the heart of sin was. He was not just responsible to conform to the world's standards around him. He was rather responsible to conform to God's perfect standards. God ultimately is the standard of right and wrong. It is his character that determines what actions are good and what actions are evil. So ultimately David's sin was against God. David recognized this fact and admits or confesses his sin to God.

The first roadblock in dealing with true guilt in our lives is our unwillingness to confess our sins to God. We all have the natural tendency to do what David tried to do by scheming to cover up our sinful actions. David had carefully covered his tracks so that his sin with Bathsheba would not be made public. But God, who knows all things, exposed David's sin because he knew that David could never find forgiveness and be freed from guilt unless he first faced and confessed his sin.

There are many ways to attempt a cover-up of sin. A bank robber might kill the witnesses in his attempt to cover up his sin. That, in essence, is similar to what David had tried. But there are many other more subtle ways. Denying our actions; excusing our sins; blaming someone else; lying to cover our tracks; justifying ourselves - these are all ways to cover sins that people try to use every day. And some of these ways might convince others, but the trouble remains in the fact that a person knows the truth of the action in his heart. So the guilt lingers there. We must admit our sins before God for what they are in order to have any possibility of freedom from guilt.

Step #2 - Acceptance of God's Forgiveness and Cleansing:

Cleanse me with hyssop, and I will be clean; wash me, and I will be whiter than snow. Let me hear joy and gladness; let the bones you have crushed rejoice. Hide your face from my sins and blot out all my iniquity. (Psalm 51:7-9)

The Hebrew word translated *cleanse me* is literally *unsin me*. It is the word *sin* with a negative prefix attached to it. Remove the sin; grant me complete and full forgiveness. The hyssop plant was the one God commanded to be used in the Passover deliverance. Israelite families were to take the blood of their Passover lamb and paint it on the top and sides of their front doorframes with a hyssop plant. When the angel of death saw the blood framing the door, he would pass over the house. After this time, the hyssop plant was used to sprinkle water in the ceremonial cleansing rituals of the priests.

David here was asking God to wash away and remove his sin with a willingness to accept God's forgiveness if it was granted. This is important to see for the second roadblock to being free from guilt in our lives is an unwillingness to accept the forgiveness that God offers to us.

If we confess our sin, he is faithful and just to forgive us our sin, and to cleanse us from all unrighteousness. (1 John 1:9)

Jesus Christ came as the sacrificial, Passover lamb to pay the penalty for our sins. God promises to forgive us as we admit our sins to him. But many people do not experience God's forgiveness because they are unwilling to receive it.

We all know deep inside that we have done wrong and we feel that we should pay a penalty for our sins. This is the underlying reason for many people allowing themselves to continue in the bondage to guilt. They feel that the feelings of guilt are a penance for their sins. They deserve to feel guilty after what they have done. So they continue on in their misery, unwilling to receive God's forgiveness. If we are to be freed from imprisoning guilt, we must believe that the Lord Jesus Christ paid the penalty for our sins and we must be willing to accept the forgiveness that God offers through Him.

Step #3 - Repentance:

Create in me a pure heart, O God, and renew a steadfast spirit within me. (Psalm 51:10)

Repentance also is a crucial step. Repentance is a turning away from our sin. Repentance is a commitment not to continue in our sin. Repentance is a decision to go in another direction in life. There are numbers of people who continue in the cycle of repeating the same sin over and over again because they might follow the first two steps but they never get to this third step. They sin, they feel guilty for their action, and they confess the sin before God. They might even accept his forgiveness. But they never deal with that weakness in their life so they soon repeat that same sin again.

David recognized the fact that his sin with Bathsheba revealed a weakness that he had in his life. Those lustful desires that he had deep down in his heart had to be changed. So he asked God to create in him a pure heart and to renew a steadfast spirit within him. In other words, David was willing to repent from his sinful ways and accept God's corrective measures in his life. David was willing to change his life patterns. We don't know all of the details of the changes that this involved. Perhaps David resolved to no longer take any walks on his palace roof in the cool of the evening when women normally bathed. Perhaps David set up an accountability network around him. But whatever the specifics, David repented of his sinful actions, realizing that they were conceived within the wickedness of his heart.

There is a seemingly minor detail that is given at the end of David's life that testifies to David's change of heart in this area of his life. As an old man, David had trouble with his circulation. He was always cold. So the palace officials devised a plan to make the king more comfortable. They found the most beautiful young woman that they could find and they gave her the job of keeping the King warm. She snuggled up close to him in bed at night as a portable human heater. But listen to the detail of this account as recorded in the first chapter of the Kings account.

When King David was old and well advanced in years, he could not keep warm even when they put covers over him. So his servants said to him, "Let us look for a young virgin to attend the king and take care of him. She can lie beside him so that our lord the king may keep warm." Then they searched throughout Israel for a beautiful girl and found Abishag, a Shunammite, and brought her to the king. The girl was very beautiful; she took care of the king and waited on him, but the king had no intimate relations with her. (1 Kings 1:1-4)

Men who harbor lustful thoughts in their hearts during their younger years become a slave to lust in their lives and grow up to be dirty old men. David was not this type of man. He was a man who had gained victory in this area of his life. He had repented of this type of lifestyle.

Step #4 - Concern for Relationship with God:

Do not cast me from your presence or take your Holy Spirit from me. (Psalm 51:11)

Now I mentioned earlier in this chapter that there are two difficult verses to interpret that are often misunderstood in this Psalm. The first one is verse four and we looked at that one previously. Verse 11 is the second one. This verse is often used by those who claim that true Christians can lose their salvation. *Here is a place where it is obvious that David was concerned that he might lose his salvation*, they say. But a careful examination of the text evidences this not to be the case. First of all, if David could have lost his salvation because of his sinful transgression, he already would have. He had already committed the treacherous acts. Therefore, he shouldn't have been concerned about losing his salvation here, but rather concerned with getting it back again if it were possible for a true believer to become unborn from God's family. And in the second place, the verse following this one makes it clear that David was not concerned so much with the position of his salvation than with the joy of it. *Restore to me the joy of your salvation,* he writes.

So then, if David was not referring to his positional state in God's family here, what was he talking about? Again, the cultural background helps us here. In these Old Testament days, before the Holy Spirit had come on the day of Pentecost to have that special indwelling relationship with the members of Christ's body, chosen

177

individuals were anointed by the Holy Spirit for specific offices. This was not in connection with their salvation, but rather it was for special areas of service. Specifically, chosen individuals were called to be priests, prophets and kings, and were specially anointed for those tasks. In these New Testament times, all believers are called to be priests, prophets and kings (Revelation 1:6), but this was not true in the Old Testament days.

Now David had just witnessed the former King, Saul, having that special anointing for kingship taken away from him as a result of a sin that he committed. 1 Samuel 15 gives the account of Saul's disobedience of God's command to him and Samuel's statement in response.

Because you have rejected the word of the Lord, God has rejected you as king . . . and has given it to one of your neighbors - to one better than you. (1 Samuel 15:23,28)

David was the one who was then anointed by the prophet Samuel to be the next king of Israel. David knew firsthand that a serious, willful sin could mean his rejection as king, that the Holy Spirit's anointing and power for kingship could be taken from him. So he pleaded with God that his position might not be affected by his transgression. God heard and granted David's prayer. We might ask why God granted David's request here and not King Saul's? The answer, of course, is found in the fact that Saul never followed the first three steps. He justified and rationalized his sin rather than confessing it, he did not receive God's forgiveness, and he never repented of his ways. So he was rejected as king. But David did confess his sin, he did receive God's forgiveness, and he did repent of his sinful ways. So he was allowed to continue in the position of being king.

Step #5 - The Joy of Restored Fellowship with God:

Restore to me the joy of your salvation and grant me a willing spirit, to sustain me. (Psalm 51:12)

David realized that salvation comes from the Lord. If his position were dependent upon his faithfulness, he knew that he would be doomed. So it is interesting that he doesn't ask to have the joy of his own salvation restored, but he rather asks for God to restore the joy of your salvation. David realized the truth that only God can save; and only God can sustain.

What joy and confidence this truth brings to our lives as we realize that our eternal salvation is in God's hands. But that joy is lost when we willfully sin against God. David requested that the joy of his relationship with God be restored to him so that he might feel the position that he had with the Lord once again.

Step #6 - A Concern to Strengthen Others:

Then I will teach transgressors your ways, and sinners will turn back to you. (Psalm 51:13)

179

The final step showed a concern on David's part to help others. David realized the fact that God was able to work out even the most devastating experiences in his life for his eternal good. As David learned critical lessons in his life, he would be better prepared and equipped to help others around him. So it is true that through the experiences that we have, we are able to share insights and wisdom so that others can avoid the pitfalls we have suffered. If we are wise, we can also learn from the experiences of others so that we won't have to suffer the same consequences that they had to endure. We are also able to come beside those who are struggling with similar sins and be a mentor to them to help them find the path to victory. But we can only do this as we have found that path ourselves. That is the reason for this step being at the end. After confession, after receiving forgiveness, after repentance, after the concern for the restoration of our relationship with God, even after the restoring of the joy of the Lord back into our lives, comes the perspective to help others. We must have traveled the entire path in order to help others find their way. Until we have traveled the path to restoration ourselves, our primary concern should be our own relationship with God. We must first get back into a proper fellowship with the Lord ourselves. But after that has been achieved, we then are in a position to help others find the path to victory as well. We can become spiritual guides and mentors for those who have been entrapped by the enemy or their own sinful desires.

It was a chilly night in November of 1836 when John kissed his wife and children and left home never to return to Vermont. John didn't want to leave, but both he and his family knew that he must if he were to remain a free man. The County Sheriff was coming to arrest John. So, very reluctantly, John's wife who was six months pregnant and his four daughters said *good-bye* to him, and John fled west. If John had only been a dangerous killer, it would certainly have been different. But John wasn't. He was a good family man, a hard worker, a blacksmith by trade.

Five years earlier, John at age twenty-seven had decided that it was time to open his own shop. He needed capital to work with so he accepted some money from a silent partner named Jay Wright and opened a blacksmith shop in Lester, Vermont. The town needed a good blacksmith and John was one. Well, business went very well until John's shop caught on fire one day and burned to the ground. These were the days before fire insurance so John was worse off than before. Now he no longer had a shop and he owed Wright a good sum of money.

Well, Jay Wright continued to see the potential in John and decided to stake him again. After the shop was rebuilt, John began business again. Again business prospered for a few months until the second shop caught fire and burned down. Now Wright became quite upset with John as if John had burned down two shops purposefully to put himself in a huge, financial hole. But fire was always a potentiality with the blacksmith trade for there was always a furnace roaring hot enough to melt metal.

With relationships strained, John moved to a neighboring town, the town of Hancock near John's in-laws. Well, in time, John saved enough money making springs for a carriage company to open another small blacksmith shop. It was small at first, but business soon began to pick up. John was just about in a financial position to begin to pay back Jay Wright when the lender learned of John's success and immediately jumped to the conclusion that John was trying to weasel out of his debts.

John appealed to Wright for forgiveness assuring him that all debts would be paid in full. He even agreed to set up any payment plan that Wright desired, but the lender would not hear of any agreement. No, John must pay this time. If only Wright had needed the money, but he didn't. He was one of the wealthiest men in the entire area. He was just filled with bitterness and hatred for John who had not produced for him the kind of investment that he had anticipated. So a warrant was signed out for John's arrest. John would rot in jail until every penny of the debt had been paid. That would mean a life sentence for John would have no means to pay for his debt while in jail.

It was with a heavy heart that John fled his home state of Vermont. He could not take his family with him for his wife was pregnant with their next child. He would have to flee for his life and hope to provide for his family's coming later. John ran west until he was confident that he was out of the grasp of Jay Wright. He stopped in the town of Grand Detour, Illinois. John opened a small shop there, and in time made quite a contribution to the farming community. John changed the plows of the farmers from the old fashioned, bulky iron plows that became clodded with the rich Midwestern dirt to a new, self-cleaning, steel plow. That plow made John famous. It enabled him to pay off his debt to Jay Wright, and to eventually bring his family out west to join him. And his company remains to this day.

But if John Deere would have had his preference at the time, he would have traded that plow and the fame that it brought for the pain of having to leave his family that first time when he felt forced to flee west. But he didn't feel that he could stay in Vermont because there was no heart of forgiveness there. There was no possibility of pardon from the past.

Forgiveness, pardon- these are beautiful words. Everyone is eager to know the relief of forgiveness from past mistakes. Some people even try to capitalize on this innate human desire. I recently noticed a religious mail order gimmick. It offered complete absolution from one's sins for only thirty-five dollars. That's right! All a person had to do was send thirty-five dollars to the *Church of World Peace* and he would receive a kit that completely forgave sins. And for an extra five dollars the gullible person could also obtain a *sainthood certificate*. Most amazingly, thousands of people responded sending in millions of dollars just on the chance that they might receive some relief from guilt, some measure of forgiveness.

David, the greatest King in Israel's history, knew something about God's forgiveness. We looked at David's great sin with Bathsheba in the previous chapter. The facts that he lusted after her beauty, committed adultery with her, and then tried to cover his actions by actually murdering her husband, Uriah, are not covered up by the Scriptures, but are rather openly revealed.

From a human perspective, David had performed the perfect sin, completely covered and hidden from the eyes of the people. But David was being eaten up inside by his own transgressions. And all of these feelings and emotions came bursting forth when he was confronted by Nathan the prophet.

David wrote two responses giving forth his feelings and remorse following this tragic situation with Bathsheba. They are Psalms 51 and 32. Most Bible scholars think Psalm 51 was written shortly after the Prophet Nathan confronted David. Psalm 32 was likely written some time later, after David had processed and evaluated his heinous act. Having already seen David's six step plan in Psalm 51, we now turn our attention to the blessedness of God's forgiveness revealed in Psalm 32.

Blessed is he whose transgressions are forgiven, whose sins are covered. Blessed is the man whose sin the LORD does not count against him and in whose spirit is no deceit.

When I kept silent, my bones wasted away through my groaning all day long. For day and night your hand was heavy upon me; my strength was sapped as in the heat of summer. Selah

Then I acknowledged my sin to you and did not cover up my iniquity. I said, "I will confess my transgressions to the LORD"-- and you forgave the guilt of my sin. Selah

Therefore let everyone who is godly pray to you while you may be found; surely when the mighty waters rise, they will not reach him. You are my hiding place; you will protect me from trouble and surround me with songs of deliverance. Selah

I will instruct you and teach you in the way you should go; I will counsel you and watch over you. Do not be like the horse or the mule, which have no understanding but must be controlled by bit and bridle or they will not come to you. Many are the woes of the wicked, but the LORD's unfailing love surrounds the man who trusts in him.

Rejoice in the LORD and be glad, you righteous; sing, all you who are upright in heart! (Psalm 32:1-11)

There are two main streams of thought that run through this psalm like railroad tracks across a plain. First of all, David agonizes over the seriousness of sin. But then he also extols the blessedness of forgiveness. Both of these are critical in understanding this greatest of all gifts that God offers to every person.

When we are plagued by guilt in our lives, our natural tendency is to minimize sin. We instinctively try to rationalize its seriousness away. *What we did really wasn't that bad,* we tell ourselves. *We had to do it. There are far greater sins in the world than this little one that I have committed.* We naturally think this way trying to convince ourselves that belittling our sin will somehow ease our guilt. But David's response was quite different. He emphasized the serious nature of his sin in a couple of ways.

One of these ways was the variety of terms that he used to describe his sin. The Hebrew language is rich in the vocabulary that it possesses to describe the many facetted sides of sin. There are over ten different words in the Hebrew language that are translated by our single term *sin* in one place or another in our English translations. In addition, there are also many synonymous terms that are used for sin.

In the first two verses of this Psalm, David used four different words to describe his sin. It's obvious that he was seeking to show the seriousness of sin and the dire consequences of it by the terms he used to describe it. The first term that David used was *transgressions*. This is a word that means *willful rebellion* or *mutiny*. It was a term that was often used in military contexts speaking of soldiers who would turn against their commander and fail to obey his orders in mutiny.

The second term is translated *sins*. It is the most common Hebrew term for sin corresponding to the Greek word meaning *to miss the mark*. It was a word drawn from the field of archery in Biblical times. The bow and arrow was a major military weapon in ancient days. Anyone who has ever watched an archery competition knows there is a small circle surrounded by other larger concentric circles of differing colors that comprise the bull's eye or target area. The archer must sink his arrow into that small, darkly colored circle in the middle in order to gain the maximum number of points. If he misses the mark, he loses points and likely will not win the competition. In the Olympic Games, the competition is so fierce that one can lose a medal by missing the mark just once. God's character and righteousness is pictured in the Bible as a bull's-eye. When our actions fall short of his perfect standards, we miss the mark. The nation of Israel as a whole so consistently missed God's standards that Hosea's prophecy called them a *treacherous bow* or, literally, *a bow that never shoots straight.* (Hosea 7:16)

David used another term in verse three in the original language even though the NIV also translates it *sin*. The KJV translates this word *iniquity*. The word literally means *to twist away from God's path, to pervert, to take that which is good and right and straight and make it crooked.*

The final term found in verse two is *deceit*. This means *to cover up the wickedness, to pretend that it is not there, to try to fool God, ourselves and others into thinking that we are righteous, pure and good when all the time we are harboring unrighteousness inside.* To not only sin, but then to cover up that sin thinking that we can fool others, even God himself, is what deceit is all about.

Now we can see why David used these specific terms because they together just begin to describe his actions with Bathsheba. David knew God's standards before he sinned with Bathsheba. He knew what proper conduct was for a godly man and king. But he both deliberately and out of the weakness of his nature violated God's commandments. The term *transgression* stresses the willfulness of his action.

God's commandment on moral purity had been clearly revealed to David. The seventh commandment read *thou shalt not commit adultery*. David knew that. But David had mutinied against the commands of his superior officer. He had rebelled against God. The term *sin* emphasizes more the weakness of human nature in missing the mark. David realized that he was weak in the flesh, and he freely admitted this.

But David went beyond his own actions in acknowledging the fact that the human race had perverted that which God had made straight. We had twisted that which God had made perfect. God made the human race perfect and upright, but we have deviated from God's standards and become crooked. So David had sinned not only because of his willful desires, not only because of the weakness of his flesh, but also because of his perverted sinful nature that he shared with all other humans.

And David had even gone a step further than this. He had killed Uriah in a great attempt to cover up his actions from the people of Israel and from God. He had continued to lead his people pretending that everything was fine when really he knew that he was an adulterer and murderer in his heart. He had tried to conduct business as usual in the nation of God, carefully covering his tracks, but in his heart he knew that everything was not right.

Transgression, sins, iniquity, deceit: not a pleasant set of attributes. We certainly would not want them inscribed upon our tombstones as epitaphs. Yet in many ways, they tell our story as they told David's story.

But the seriousness of sin is not only brought out in the terms used, but also in the inner results suffered. David pulls the curtain on the inner agony that he had suffered in the next two verses.

When I kept silent, my bones wasted away through my groaning all day long. For day and night your hand was heavy upon me; my strength was sapped as in the heat of summer. (Psalm 32:3,4)

These verses scarcely need commentary. As we read them, we can feel the inner guilt and pain endured with David. David had become totally unproductive. No rest at night; no work during the day. Worry derailed his train of concentration. Guilt sapped all of his energies. His physical health had become affected. It is interesting that today modern science is emphasizing the direct correlation between emotional, spiritual and physical problems. For instance, doctors often speak of the connection between stress and digestive or heart problems.

The Bible has spoken of these all along, and here is a clear example. David, a gifted and experienced leader, was completely immobilized because of his inner anxiety and guilt. The cover-up had been perfect from a human perspective. The people of Israel would never know. But David couldn't fool himself. He knew that he was guilty of adultery and murder, and he just couldn't live at peace with himself.

Like David, we need to see the seriousness and consequences of sin. Many times we suffer greatly simply because we have taken sin too lightly, or because we are not willing to admit it completely. Oh, we are often willing to confess sin in general terms. We are willing to admit that we are weak as all people are weak by nature and that we miss the mark out of this weakness. After all, we are only human. But the manner in which we confess our sin often places the burden of the blame on God, as if to say, *you are the one who made us so weak; why did you do this to us?* Are we willing to admit our mutiny and willful rebellion against him? That's harder, isn't it? Are we willing to confess our deceit, our cover-ups, or do we just rationalize them away? David was willing to be perfectly honest before God, to accept God's evaluation of his actions, to accept his own responsibility before Him.

But David also knew the joy and relief of forgiveness. You see the whole purpose of bringing out these sins and the results of these sins in this Psalm is not just to give a public confession, but rather to focus on the second major theme: forgiveness. We will never know the complete joy and relief of forgiveness until we first experience honest and true confession. And David knew this principle.

David began this Psalm with the term *blessed* or *happy*. So it is necessary to look also at the variety of terms that David used to emphasize the glory of God's forgiveness as well. The word *forgiven* in verse one means *to take away*. It views sin as a burden to be removed. I have the job of taking out the garbage in our family. I take the cans to the curb and men come and load their contents into trucks, taking the garbage to the county landfill. The garbage is removed from my sight, my mind, and my responsibility. So it is that God removes our sin as far as the east is from the west to be remembered against us no longer. This is forgiveness.

The second term is *covered*. David had tried to conceal his sin through deceit. But the stain had leaked through and made its ugly appearance again. David had been unable to cover his sin. But upon David's confession to God, God had covered his sin. And when God covers a sin, it is put out of sight permanently. The ugly stain can never leak through again for it has been covered by the shed blood of Jesus Christ himself.

The third word that David used was a legal term or one that a bookkeeper might use. It is translated *not counted*. It means to not be reckoned, or not be accredited to an account. On God's great ledger, the sin is removed from our account and it is credited to Christ's account, paid for in full by His death upon the cross.

All of these glorious results of forgiveness were given to David upon the confession of his sin to God. The same can be true in our lives. And we must notice this for the central theme of this Psalm is both the seriousness of sin and the forgiveness of God. Sin is terrible. It comes in all shapes and sizes. It can catch us unaware or we sometimes walk right into it with our eyes wide open. But it always clutches us in a hundred different strangle holds and threatens to pin our backs to the mat. But the power of God's forgiveness is greater than the power of sin. There is no sin that God cannot cleanse. There is no life that he cannot turn from misery and frustration to fruitfulness and satisfaction. God is a forgiving God. We had better never forget that. God forgives on the basis of our honest and frank confession, our admission of guilt.

David concludes this psalm with some beautiful results of God's forgiveness. We have already seen the results of sin in David's life, but look at **two wonderful results** of God's priceless forgiveness.

The first is **security**. Do you long to be accepted and secure forever?   God's forgiveness brings this wonderful confidence into a person's life.

You are my hiding place; you will protect me from trouble and surround me with songs of deliverance. (Psalm 32:7)

The second result is **guidance**. Do you sometimes feel like you are going around in circles? Do you long for a concrete direction in life, guidance for the future? God's forgiveness brings consistent direction into a person's life.

I will instruct you and teach you in the way you should go; I will counsel you and watch over you. (Psalm 32:8)

We can only imagine the relief that filled the heart of Richard Nixon on that historic day, September 9, 1974, when President Gerald Ford uttered the words granting him a *free, full and absolute pardon*. The cover-up of Watergate had brought such pain and misery to his life. One look at the deep wrinkles in his face showed that he had aged many years during those last few months before his resignation from the presidency. Now he didn't have to live in the fear that one day some secret servicemen would show up at his door in California to take him away to prison.

But Richard Nixon's relief was nothing compared to David's relief because a president of the United States can only pardon prison sentences for criminal offenses. He cannot relieve the inner sense of guilt and pain. But God can. God's pardons are complete. He removes our sins as far as the east is from the west to be remembered against us no longer. Our God is a forgiving God. The cross is the guarantee. His word is his pledge. The experience of David is the evidence. And we can have the same measure of forgiveness, no matter how many or how serious our sins.

THE COUP D' ETAT
Chapter 15

Human history often turns on seemingly fragile hinges.   Small events sometimes bring about great consequences.   One cannot help but wonder how the history of the former Soviet Union and the world it affected would have been changed if Leon Trotsky would have succeeded Vladimir Lenin instead of the ruthless Joseph Stalin. Trotsky was the logical choice. He had been Lenin's right hand man.   He had been the one largely responsible for the early stability of the socialist regime.

But when Vladimir Lenin died in 1924, the cruel Stalin quickly grabbed power. He recognized Trotsky as his chief rival and began to hunt him down like an animal. Trotsky ran from country to country seeking exile, but nobody welcomed him.   Finally, Leon found a home in Mexico City where he built an imposing fortress with a fifteen foot brick wall and guard houses. He would wait until the time was right and then return to Russia to take what should be rightfully his.

But Joseph Stalin was not a man to leave an enemy alone. That very summer, a man who called himself Frank Jackson showed up at Trotsky's fortress. In reality, he was one of Stalin's assassins.   Through convincing lies, he gained Leon's confidence.   And then in an unguarded moment, he drove a mountaineer's pick ax through the back of Trotsky's head. The coup d' etat was complete. Joseph Stalin was in full power. The nation of Russia, many surrounding nations that would be annexed, and the whole world would suffer decades of terror because of one man's lust for power.

A coup d' etat is an unsettling experience for any country. When somebody tries to wrest control from the established authority, everybody gets nervous. There are many questions left unanswered for a time. What kind of government are we going to have now? How will the new leadership affect me and my family? Will the change bring about prosperity or chaos and anarchy?

In the last couple of chapters, we have looked at the spiritual and moral low-point in the life of King David. We have seen how David was able to find restoration in his fellowship with God and get back on track spiritually again.

In the next two chapters, we want to look at the political low-point in the life of King David. Up to this point, David has known nothing but political success. He ascended to the throne when it was almost not worth having, for to be the king of Israel just meant a bulls-eye had been painted on his chest for the Philistines. But by courageous leadership and skillful administrative skills, David had quickly built a great nation. He won battle after battle. He subdued nation after nation.

Soon, the nation of Israel was no longer the doormat of the Middle East. Now, large quantities of gold and silver were pouring in annual tribute. Even David's spiritual struggles hadn't appeared to hinder the growth of the empire. While David was struggling internally back in Jerusalem, Joab was leading the army in defeating the Ammonites. So David had really never known political defeat. He had never known political defeat until the coup d' etat happened.

Now it is amazing that this coup could have gotten off of the ground in the first place. After all, the nation of Israel had never been in better shape politically. Why would Israelites back a plan to try to overthrow the man who had done so much for their nation? And the leader of the coup was Absalom, David's own son. But as amazing as it seems, it happened. David had slowly lost touch with the pulse of his subjects as his kingdom had expanded and he had more and more administrative concerns.

Absalom had slowly won the hearts of many as he listened to their problems and concerns with a sympathetic ear. Finally, Absalom had been able to organize a large enough band of willing followers to drive King David from his royal residence in Jerusalem and, for a period of time, Absalom became the functional king of the nation of Israel.

David wrote two psalms that are found back to back in our English Bibles responding to this humiliating episode in his life. They are Psalms 3 and 4.

Psalm 3 was likely written very shortly after King David was driven from the city of Jerusalem. Many Bible scholars feel there is a distinct possibility that this Psalm was written on the very morning of the battle between David's army and Absalom's renegades. This would be the conflict that would determine the future of the nation of Israel.

Psalm 3 is divided into **three distinct sections**. Each section concludes with the word *Selah.* This Hebrew term means *to pause and reflect*. It was likely used as either a pause in the reading of the Psalm or a pause in the singing of the Psalm where there would be a musical interlude by the instruments.

The theme that weaves through this Psalm like a thread is **FEAR**. This certainly should not surprise anyone for fear would be expected to be the dominant emotion of a king who had just been deposed from his throne and who was running for his life. Now the emotion of fear was hardly a new one for David. He undoubtedly experienced fear as a young lad when he was tending his father's sheep and looked around to see a lion or a bear lurking about the camp. We know that he killed both of these animals for he told King Saul his exploits.

He certainly experienced fear as a teenager when he chose to face the giant Goliath. There must have at least been the thought that flashed into David's mind as he was beginning his walk out to meet Goliath - *what have I gotten myself into now?* We know that David faced the emotion of fear many times as he was running from King Saul as a young man in his twenties for he wrote about his anxious feelings in other Psalms.

But the fear that David faced now as an older man was different. Before, as a younger man, he had everything to gain and nothing to lose. He could afford to take risks, big risks, without much to lose because he really didn't have anything. But at this later time in his life, just the opposite was true. David had been the king for several decades now. He had built the empire up into a formidable force. Now, he had everything to lose. He

196

could lose his throne, his international reputation, his family, his wealth and his life. And even if he won this battle against Absalom and his army, he would probably lose his son and go back into the city of Jerusalem having been greatly humbled. No wonder David was filled with fear. He didn't know what the future held for him or for his dearly loved nation. As we have now seen many times, David provides a wonderful example in facing the practical difficulties of life. He was a man after God's own heart. And in Psalm 3, we find a powerful model in facing fear successfully.

Now none of us has the exact same fears that David faced here. None of us is a king or queen of a country. None of us is anticipating fighting a life and death battle with swords and spears this next week. But we surely do have struggles that generate the emotion of fear in our lives. Every parent has faced the fear of a child who chooses a destructive path in life like David's son Absalom did here. And most of us have laid our heads down on our pillows and tried to sleep with the awareness that we will have to face a major struggle the next day. Perhaps that struggle will take place in a surgeon's operating room; perhaps that struggle will take place in our boss' office at work; perhaps that struggle will take place in a classroom where we will take that final exam. But whatever our particular struggle, we have to successfully win the victory over fear first if we are to have the opportunity to be at our best in the battles of life. David models facing fear victoriously in Psalm 3.

The first segment of this Psalm shows David's willingness to face his fears honestly.

O LORD, how many are my foes! How many rise up against me? Many are saying of me, "God will not deliver him." Selah (Psalm 3:1,2)

Now David was in trouble here politically, and he knew it. Absalom had been able to muster a formidable army around his mutinous cause. Later on in this Psalm, David spoke of tens of thousands who were his adversaries. If this Psalm were written on the very day of the critical battle as many believe, David realized that he had a formidable task ahead of him.   And it must have hurt him deeply that many of his fellow countrymen for whom he had risked so much in the past would have now joined the opposition against him.

But in addition to the mere numbers of his opponents, their reasoning really bothered David as well. He mentions his chagrin in the second verse. They were saying *God is no longer with David*. God's blessing has departed from David. God is no longer on David's side. How these rumors must have hurt that man who is called *the man after God's own heart.*

Now David could have responded to this threat in many ways. He could have chosen to live in the past, glorying in all of the victories that he had already achieved. He could have surrounded himself with *yes men* who would just bolster his ego and confidence and deny the realities of the surrounding threats.   But David didn't choose any of these self-deceiving paths. He freely admitted the danger that he was in and the fear that he felt.

Many people never have the opportunity to gain the victory because they won't first admit the reality of the enemy. Many people continue with addictions that greatly hinder their lifestyle because they deny that there is any problem. Many families are more willing to continue in a dysfunctional lifestyle than they are to face the reality of a problem. Many individuals are hindered in their own personal growth and achievement because they will not admit or face weaknesses in their lives. It is really fear in each case that imprisons them. The first step that David took was to admit and face the fear that must be overcome.

The second segment of this Psalm reveals the fact that **David did not allow his feelings of fear to immobilize him,** but he rather chose to put his trust in the delivering power of the Lord.

But you are a shield around me, O LORD; you bestow glory on me and lift up my head. To the LORD I cry aloud, and he answers me from his holy hill. Selah (Psalm 3:3,4)

As the great General David is thinking of the critical battle of the day, his mind begins to think in military metaphors.

*The Lord was a shield to protect him from all surrounding danger. How important the shield was in

David's day. It was the major protection that a soldier had in battle. He would use the shield both to deflect the arrows that were shot at him and the spears that were thrust at him. The shield was the soldier's only means to catch the wielded sword of the enemy in hand-to-hand combat. Just as the shield was an indispensable part of the soldier's armor, so David confesses the Lord to be his shield, both physically and spiritually.

*The Lord was the giver of glory. The Hebrew term *glory* literally means *heavy.* Again, it has military connotations. When the troops left for battle, they travelled light so as not to wear themselves out. But if they were successful, they returned heavy. They returned with large portions of gold and silver and other plunder that they had captured from their defeated enemies. They returned with glory. We give glory to God when we make him heavy with our praise and our adoration. David here expressed the confidence that God was going to give the victory to him and bring glory upon him once again.

*The Lord was also the one who could replace his shame and humiliation with honor again. David said the Lord would lift up his head. The picture is of a child who has come back into the house after a particularly humiliating experience. Perhaps he has fallen off his bike and skinned his knee or been punched in the nose by a neighborhood bully. His head is down in shame and humiliation. But what does the parent do? The parent puts a hand under that chin, lifts up his head, wipes the tears from his eyes and tells him it's going to be alright. That's what David felt God was doing for him here in this

Psalm. It must have been such a humiliating experience for David to be driven from his throne and capital city by his own flesh and blood. But it's as if God lifted up his head and said, *it's going to be alright David.*

God was personally concerned with David's predicament and always ready to hear and answer his prayer. *To the Lord I cry aloud, and he answers me from his holy hill.*

While freely admitting his dangerous situation and the fear that he was feeling, David chose to put his trust in the Lord who was the only one who could help him at this time. He acknowledged the Lord as his protector, the Lord as the only one who could return his throne and glory to him, the Lord as the one who could lift up his head and the Lord who was personally concerned for his situation.

So the first segment of this Psalm shows David's willingness to admit his difficult situation and the second segment emphasizes his choice to put his trust in the Lord. **In the third segment**, David testifies to some of the results that occurred in his life because of the decision that he had made to trust in the Lord.

I lie down and sleep; I wake again, because the LORD sustains me. I will not fear the tens of thousands drawn up against me on every side. Arise, O LORD! Deliver me, O my God! Strike all my enemies on the jaw; break the teeth of the wicked. From the LORD comes deliverance. May your blessing be on your people. Selah (Psalm 3:5-8)

The first result that David spoke about here is **sleep**. What a practical blessing this was from the Lord. A good night's sleep. And when we consider the historical setting, David's statement here is even more remarkable. The verb tenses used here indicate that the sleep has already happened, probably the night before. Now if it was true that this Psalm was written on the morning of the day of battle with Absalom's forces, it is certainly noteworthy that David had experienced a good night's sleep the previous night.

It would not have been natural for him to have a sound sleep the night before such a critical battle. He had been sleeping on the ground somewhere in a cave rather than in his own bed in the palace. He had fallen asleep with all of the attempted coup anxieties heavy on his mind. But even if this wasn't the very night before the battle, any good night's sleep in his unsettling circumstances would have been unusual. But David was able to sleep because he had put his trust in the Lord. David knew that God was awake, so he could sleep.

The second result was **serenity**. *I will not fear the tens of thousands drawn up against me on every side. (Psalm 3:6)*

The situation was still dangerous. But God had freed David from his fear. So David could respond to the situation with clarity of thought and action. Someone has said, *God doesn't promise to always change our circumstances, but he does promise to always change us.* David experienced this truth in his life. The battle still had to be fought, but he could engage in it without debilitating fear.

A third result was **salvation**. *Arise, O Lord. Deliver me, O my God. (Psalm 3:7a)* God is a saving God. God has made the provision for eternal salvation through the sacrifice of his one and only Son, the Lord Jesus Christ. God continues to offer his salvation throughout our life as we face our dangerous circumstances in his strength and power. But that salvation is only experienced as we face our fears realistically and put our faith and trust in Him. We can then have the freedom to sleep and to have God's serenity and salvation.

Helen Keller remains one of the most remarkable people in human history. Although she was both visually and hearing impaired, she learned how to read and communicate with others. Eventually, Helen Keller would write fluently and with keen understanding. One characteristic of Helen's life that enabled her to achieve so much more than anyone ever thought she could was her courage to face life's fears. The following is a quote from Peter Seymour's book entitled, *Courage.*

When Helen Keller, in front of the lion cage at the zoo, said she was going inside to get better acquainted, she was told it was absolutely impossible. This particular lion was tough, just in from Africa. But Helen gave reasons for her desire to go inside. She had been studying all she could about lions and was sure she could manage. Somehow, she got her way. The lion was surprised. He had never seen a human being like this one. Of course, he couldn't understand that here was a famous woman who

203

was not only blind. She was deaf as well. But he could sense perhaps that she had the gift of empathy, of identifying herself with other creatures. Anyway, as she stretched out her hands inquiringly and started walking directly toward him, he offered no resistance.

In front of him, she kneeled with a sort of contagious reverence for the way he was put together. Down his back she ran her sensitive fingers. Yes, the mane was just as the books had described it and so was the fur on the tail. But what was this at the very end? This tuft of long hairs. Nobody had mentioned that. "How interesting", she chuckled. The exploring touch went down one leg to the paw. The lion cooperatively lifted it. She felt the claws, one after the other, then the pad, up and down.

"Here, that's enough", said the lion with a great roar. But Helen Keller couldn't hear although the vibrations must have startled her. Showing no shock or anxiety, she continued testing each paw and leg muscle. Finally, satisfied, she stood up and lifted her hands in a gesture of wonder and admiration. Taking her time, she found her way to the door of the cage and rejoined her friends who were once more breathing freely.

Most people would consider being in an enclosed cage with an African lion to be a threatening experience. I know I would. Most people would be frozen with fear. Most people wouldn't remember much at all about the experience except for the times waking up screaming after having a nightmare. But then none would have experienced the exhilaration that Helen Keller did by actually coming into physical contact with the King of Beasts.

Whatever fears we face, we must allow God to give us freedom in order for life to be an exhilarating experience.

*Like David, we must face our fears courageously. We must be willing to admit them.

*Like David, we must choose to trust in the Lord. God is greater than any life-threatening situation.

*Like David, we must accept his divine gifts of sleep, serenity and salvation into our lives.

RELIEF FROM STRESS
Chapter 16

There was tension in the air as the men representing their fellow citizens from thirteen different colonies met in Philadelphia on that summer morning in 1776. These were ordinary men who had achieved a measure of security through their ingenuity and hard work. Some were lawyers; some were merchants; some were farmers. All were respected by their neighbors for they had been sent to Philadelphia as representatives. For over a year now conflict had been raging with the mother country. Many good men on both sides had already died. The rift that had developed was now so wide and deep that most felt there was no turning back. So on the second day of July a vote was taken to declare independence from Great Britain. A new country had been born.

Two days later, on July 4th, a Declaration of Independence was confirmed. Fifty-six men signed that document pledging to each other *our lives, our fortunes, and our sacred honor.* This was not an idle commitment that these men made. Some of these men would die in the war of independence; others would be captured and imprisoned by the British; still others would lose their homes and fortunes. Every single man would make a significant sacrifice. Each man would endure intense stress. For whenever there is a major change, there is always the stress that accompanies that change. And when a government is changed, there can't help but be many questions that produce stress. *What will the new government be like? How will my life and family be affected? Will life be better or worse after the new government is formed?*

Happily, this new government that formed the United States of America worked out better than anyone could have envisioned. But there were many times when nobody knew that this would be the case. And there certainly are countless examples of government changes in human history that ended up with disastrous results. There have been communist revolutions, Nazi regimes, and brutal dictatorships that have massacred millions of innocent people. So a change in government status puts everyone on edge. During this time there's always a great deal of tension and stress on everyone involved.

None of us is unaware of the stresses involved in living. The very word *stress* is one of the most unpopular terms in our vocabulary today. Doctors continually speak of stress and the toll that it takes on our physical health. Employers speak of stress and the productivity that it costs the company. Our families tell us that stress is robbing them of quality time. We all know that stress is certainly among the top ten on the public enemy list.

Yet knowledge of the problem does not often seem to help with its remedy. In spite of our awareness, the stresses of life continue to escalate. Our lives become more harried, our work less productive, and our families more frustrated or, worse yet, apathetic.

It is of some comfort to us to realize that our generation is not the only one that has dealt with stress.

Sometimes we think that's the case because of the emphasis that is placed upon stress today, but that assumption is not true.

David suffered periods in his life under great stress, and he often referred to this problem in the psalms. Psalm 4 addresses this issue. It was written during a time when David was experiencing an attempted coup. Of course, we would not expect that all of the answers to this problem of stress would be addressed in these eight brief verses, for this issue is far too complex for that kind of unrealistic expectation. But we can and do expect some helpful principles in dealing with stress in our lives and David certainly doesn't disappoint us.

Answer me when I call to you, O my righteous God. Give me relief from my distress; be merciful to me and hear my prayer.

How long, O men, will you turn my glory into shame? How long will you love delusions and seek false gods? Know that the LORD has set apart the godly for himself; the LORD will hear when I call to him. In your anger do not sin; when you are on your beds, search your hearts and be silent. Offer right sacrifices and trust in the LORD. Many are asking, "Who can show us any good?"

Let the light of your face shine upon us, O LORD. You have filled my heart with greater joy than when their grain and new wine abound. I will lie down and sleep in peace, for you alone, O LORD, make me dwell in safety. (Psalm 4:1-8)

Psalm 4 falls naturally into three major sections. In the first verse, David's problem is stated; in verses two through the first part of verse six, the reasons for his problem are found; and then in the last three verses, some helpful suggestions in dealing with the problem are discovered.

David's problem simply stated in the first verse is the problem of stress. *Give me relief from my distress,* he cried out to God.

Now the historical setting of this Psalm is critical in understanding the stress that David was under at this point in his life. In the previous chapter, we saw the fact that Psalm 4 was one of two Psalms that were written by King David immediately after Absalom had attempted his coup of the throne. These Psalms are found back to back in our English Bibles.

Psalm 3 was likely written very shortly after King David fled the city of Jerusalem. The theme that is woven through Psalm 3 like a thread is **FEAR**. Psalm 3 revealed how threatened David felt personally. This Psalm was probably written before Psalm 4 on the very morning of Joab's battle with Absalom's army. David was fearful of what would happen that day; he was fearful for the future of the nation of Israel; he was fearful for himself personally. This was the conflict that would determine the future of the nation of Israel. But David was able to overcome his personal fears with courage and take back the throne that God had given to him.

In Psalm 4, David speaks of the tremendous **STRESS** under which he was functioning. Even though this Psalm, unlike the previous one, does not have an historical subtitle linking it to Absalom's coup, most Bible scholars do link it to this time in David's life for two reasons. First, the content of this Psalm fits into this period in David's life. And second, this fourth Psalm historically has been connected with the third Psalm. The two Psalms are even joined together in some ancient manuscripts. Because the third Psalm clearly does give the historical setting in its inscription, it would only be natural to assume that same historical setting for Psalm 4 as well. And the two Psalms certainly complement each other thematically, for fear and stress would be the two major emotions that any king would experience during a time when somebody was trying to usurp his throne. Without doubt, this setting in David's life was one of the most stressful times that he ever endured.

The original language that is used in the first verse is most interesting for it paints a military picture in the mind of the reader. C.H. Spurgeon in his *Treasury of David* says of this verse, it presents *a figure taken from an army enclosed in a field, and hardly pressed by the surrounding enemy. God hath dashed down the rocks and given me room; he hath broken the barriers and set me in a large place.* David felt that he was pinned in by the opposing forces. He felt trapped in a canyon with mountains on each side, with no place to turn. So he pleaded with God to give him some route of escape, some unknown tunnel, some relief from his distress.

Stresses have a way of smothering us in life. We feel trapped with no way of escape. It is interesting that this sense is even found in the derivation of the word *stress*. Our English term comes from the Latin *strictus* that means to *draw tight or compress.* That is what stress does to us in life. It makes us feel almost claustrophobic, like we are being pressed upon by all kinds of demands. This was David's problem. Having fled from his throne with the knowledge that Absalom was now ruling from Jerusalem with the hearts of the people behind him, David felt there was no hope, no place to turn, no way of escape. He was suffering under great distress.

The **reasons for David's stress** are clearly stated in the next five verses. These are worthy of note because the reasons that David gave here would not be the ones that we would naturally guess. We would think that David's stress would have come from his physical danger. After all, Absalom had an impressive army behind him, and he was going to come after David seeking to exterminate his own father as his rival once and for all. But David was not really that concerned with Absalom's military presence here. A military battle was something that David could handle, and one that he had experienced many times. A physical conflict was black and white; there was a winner and a loser, a victor and a conquered foe. This kind of clear cut event was not as difficult for a man like David to handle.

Notice the factors that David mentioned that were bringing stress into his life.

*humiliation - *how long, O men, will you turn my glory into shame? (Psalm 4:2a)* David had gone from being King of the most powerful nation in the Middle East to being a hunted fugitive. The humiliation of this experience is pictured in Shimei throwing rocks at him as he was forced to leave the city of Jerusalem in shame.

*slander - *how long will you love delusions and seek false gods? (Psalm 4:2b)* Absalom's greatest tool in dethroning his father had been his slanderous tongue. Sitting by the city gate, he had degraded his father, the king, claiming that he would do this or that to help the people. You can promise everyone everything if you don't have to deliver. Those who are out of power have a great advantage in that they can make great promises without ever having to deliver on them, and then they can criticize every step that the one in power is making. That is exactly what Absalom had done. The Bible says that he had stolen the peoples' hearts away from David with his deceitful and slanderous tongue. And now as David had fled from the palace, the rumors and the gossip increased and spread. These caused great stress in David's life for he was a man who loved honesty, truth and integrity.

*anger - *in your anger, do not sin. (Psalm 4:4)* How easy it would have been for David to boil with anger and frustration over all of these injustices that he had endured. And this natural tendency to seek personal revenge, not for the good of the nation or for God's program, but just for his own personal satisfaction, caused stress in his life especially when he was lying on his bed at night and his mind mulled over all of the events of the past days.

*gloom and despair - *many are asking, who can show us any good? (Psalm 4:6a)* David's friends weren't helping him much. Instead of encouraging, they were just

212

reaffirming that everything had fallen apart, that there was no hope for the future now, no light at the end of the tunnel to be seen. Perhaps this sense of hopelessness, not being able to see any way out of the situation, brings the most stress of all into life.

So then David was under great stress, perhaps greater stress than any of us have ever felt. He was the King over God's people, responsible before God for the stability and direction of the nation. And now, he had been driven from his throne. The nation was in utter turmoil without a recognized leader, and his own son Absalom was seeking his life.

In addition to everything else, he had been totally humiliated, people were slandering him and telling all kinds of lies about him, he was battling frustration and vengeful thoughts in his own mind, and everyone around him seemed to be painting a picture of doom and gloom. What a depressing picture! But that is what stress can do. If it is allowed to rule supreme, stress can completely turn a person's life upside down.

Happily, David's life did not end in this state. He was able to once again gain control of the throne. The rival forces were conquered. And he lived many more productive years, dying at an old age, full of accomplishments, and loved by his nation as a godly king. Part of the reason for his success was the fact that David was able to deal with stress productively in his life.

In this Psalm, David gives **three remedies** in the final three verses to the stresses that he was feeling. These are not meant to be three quick and easy magical formulas to remove all stress from life. David certainly never meant for them to be the final answers for stress and he continued to deal with stress throughout his own life. But they were helpful to David, and they will also help us if we will put them into practice.

First of all, David **maintained his fellowship with the Lord** in the midst of his stresses. *Let the light of your face shine upon us, O LORD. (Psalm 4:6b)* Now this is very critical to mention because, when stresses come upon us, when we feel hemmed in on every side, when our time and energies are at a premium, the first temptation that we face is to cut out of our schedule that which is not urgent, that which doesn't have to be done right at this moment. Among the first items to go can be our daily quiet time with the Lord in meditation and prayer. After all, we rationalize, we just don't have time for Bible reading today; we don't have time for prayer. We have too many other things that just can't wait, that must be done.

When we rob ourselves of our quiet times with the Lord, we increase our problems. We hurt ourselves for several reasons. First of all, totally apart from any spiritual value whatsoever, our daily quiet time with the Lord is of great value to us physically because it is a time when we break from the hectic schedule of life and have a segment of time in quiet meditation. This, in itself, is of great value in combating stress. But more importantly, we must recognize that our greatest helper in the battle against stress is the Lord himself. So when we fail to spend time with him, we cut ourselves off from our source of help, we sever ourselves from our greatest ally. He is the one who is able to clothe us with the shoes of peace. He is the one who is able to help soothe our anxieties. He is the one who is able to give us a proper perspective on the situation.

So then, when we feel greatly distressed, one of the first questions that we should ask ourselves is *am I spending regular time with the Lord in reading his Word and praying? Is the light of his face shining upon me in fellowship?* David realized the importance of maintaining fellowship with God. After all, he took the time to write this Psalm in the midst of this very stressful situation. So too, we will be helped as we remember to engage in times of meditation and prayer.

But David also **maintained other proper priorities** in the midst of his stresses as well. *You have filled my heart with greater joy than when their grain and new wine abound. (Psalm 4:7)* David had potentially lost a great deal in material possessions as he was writing this Psalm. David was a wealthy man at this time in his life. Yet, potentially and probably from his perspective, David had lost his palatial home, all of his gold and silver reserves, tribute and tax money that would annually come in, and all of his material possessions in the world. Rather than bemoaning his losses, however, David confessed that the joy that God gave into his heart was far greater than an abundance of grain and wine. Maintaining proper priorities helped David deal with life's stresses.

I am convinced that many stresses are brought on us because our priorities are out of whack. We look with covetous eyes at what our neighbor has when the Bible clearly says in the tenth commandment that we are not to covet our neighbor's wealth. And then we place ourselves in bondage in order to accumulate these material things that we could easily live without and usually cannot afford. And from that point on we bring stress after stress into our lives. Dads have to work more hours to maintain and to expand material possessions, bringing personal stress and family stress. Many moms are working long hours simply to provide the extra material things, not necessities, causing a breakdown in family relationships and insecurity among children. Our lives are filled with stressful schedules, and instead of simplifying our lives, we try to solve the problem by taking on more. And we pay for our improper priorities. Stress is one of the major bills.

Now it is God's will that we work hard. And every person has different tolerance levels so we certainly cannot set one model up as ideal for all family situations. What is God's will for one family might not be God's will for another family. And we all go through periods in our life when we have to temporarily endure that which is not ideal. But within our own stress tolerations, we must each search our hearts to make sure that our priorities are really proper so that we are not bringing added stresses upon ourselves. David was a King with all of the fame, wealth and glory that went along with that position. Yet he admitted that joy in his heart was worth more than material prosperity. Yes, David was under a great deal of stress. But at least he didn't compound his problem by adding improper priorities.

In the third place, **David sought to maintain adequate rest.** *I will lie down and sleep in peace, for you alone, O LORD, make me dwell in safety. (Psalm 4:8)*

Have you ever wondered why God made us so that we need to have rest and sleep at night? After all, sleep appears to waste a third of our lives. If a person lives an average lifespan of seventy-five years, approximately twenty-five of those years will be spent in the unconscious state of sleep. God didn't have to design life this way. He could have created us like a battery with the capacity to run for seventy-five years before losing power. Perhaps one reason for God creating humans to need sleep was that he knew rest would help people cope better with stress?

If anyone had justification for staying up all night worrying about the state of the nation it would have been David. He had just been deposed as King. What was going to happen to his nation? His life was on the line. The world was falling apart. Yet he affirmed that he would trust in the Lord and then would lie down and get a good night's rest. In other words, David was careful to take care of himself physically.

Very seldom is anything constructively achieved by staying up all night worrying. Usually, the matter is bigger and more complicated the next day and we are too exhausted to think clearly. We need rest. It is also helpful to get away from pressures by having physical exercise and proper nutrition to help our bodies be strengthened. Days off that are really days off can make our work more productive. Not just days stewing about our problems at home, but days away from work's stresses can refresh us. Vacations. Even short breaks of rest for the mind and body. Physical recreation. These are very important in our lives and must not be overlooked. But like our quiet time with the Lord, time off is something that is not urgent, so it can be continually put off to our own detriment.

So then David gives to us **three principles** helpful in dealing with stress. Maintain our fellowship with God so that we don't cut ourselves off from our source of help. Maintain proper priorities in our life so that we don't complicate and worsen our stressful situation needlessly. Maintain proper rest so that we will be sure that we are keeping the balance in our physical and emotional lives that God intended for us to have.

Stress can be a wonderful spice to our lives. We just need to be sure that we don't spoil the taste of the food by seasoning it too much.

When George McCluskey's first daughter was born, he felt the burden of raising a godly woman in the difficult days in which he was living. Realizing his own inadequacies as a parent, George made a commitment to pray every day for his daughter. He would thank God for the healthy girl that God had entrusted to him, and pray that God would work in her life to make her a woman of God. In time, God added a second daughter to the McCluskey household, and George included her on his prayer list as well, thanking God for her every day and praying that God would make her a godly woman.

George McCluskey prayed every day for his two daughters. And eventually they both received the Lord Jesus Christ as their personal Savior, and grew up to be women of great character and faith. Both of these women married men who went into full-time Christian service for the Lord and eventually had families of their own. Together, they brought four girls and one boy into the world as grandchildren for George McCluskey. And as each one was born, George added the new grandchild to his prayer list.

By now, George was praying a full hour each day, from eleven in the morning until noon, thanking God for those committed to his care and praying for the continued spiritual growth of his two daughters, their husbands and his five grandchildren. The five grandchildren all grew up to commit their lives to the Lord Jesus Christ. All four of the female grandchildren married men who were in full-time Christian work and the single grandson became a pastor.

The first two children born to the next generation as great grandchildren were both boys, cousins born in the same year. George McCluskey faithfully put them on his prayer list and prayed for these two great grandchildren every day. These two boys in time also received the Lord Jesus Christ as their personal Savior and committed their lives to following his will. After these cousins graduated from high school, they decided that they would go to the same college. It was during their sophomore years, that one cousin felt called to the gospel ministry.

The other cousin felt the Lord leading in a different direction. He had an interest in the field of psychology. He admitted feeling somewhat guilty because all of his relatives back to his great grandfather had gone into some kind of full-time Christian work. But he knew in his heart that God wanted him to go into the field of psychology. And that, after all, was what his great grandfather had prayed, for him to follow God's leading in his life.

Eventually, this great grandson of George McCluskey, who had been prayed for four generations, earned his doctor's degree and became the Chairman of the Pediatrics department at the University of California School of Medicine and the Director of Behavioral Research in the Division of Child Development at the Children's Hospital of Los Angeles. And interestingly enough, the books that he has written and his radio program that has spanned our nation have been the most visible source of encouragement and support for Christian families of all of George McCluskey's descendants. But we must never forget that the ministry of Dr. James Dobson, founder of Focus on the Family, that has impacted our country so much started in the prayer room of a godly great grandfather who continuously thanked God for his blessings and faithfully prayed every day for his children, grandchildren and great grandchildren.

It is impossible to calculate the impact on future generations and the course of world events that a single person can have if that person is committed to obeying God, has a grateful spirit and is a person of devotion and prayer. David was a person who had these qualities. He lived some three thousand years ago, but babies are still named after him, one of the most important cities in the world still claims to be his city, military academies still study his battle plans, and Christians who are committed to growing in their relationship with God still study his life.

This book has been devoted to studying the life of David through some of the Psalms that he wrote. We have not been able to look at all of the seventy-three psalms that we believe he authored, but we have seen many lessons that he learned in life from both victories and failures that he experienced.

In this chapter, we want to look at a characteristic of David that greatly attributed to his success in life. In fact, I believe this characteristic to be one of the major reasons for David being able to achieve so much in journeying from the shepherd's tent to the palace throne. David was a man who generally had a grateful spirit. Now

I am not claiming that David never felt depressed or angry or sorry for himself. We have already looked at Psalms that picture David in these states. But these were not characteristic of David's general attitude. They were the exception, not the rule for David's life. Generally speaking, David was a person who was filled with thanksgiving towards God. He never lost the wonder of his being chosen to be King of Israel. He didn't take his position for granted. He didn't allow the pressures of the throne to make him become cynical or bitter.

Most Bible scholars list Psalm 103 among David's last works. In this Psalm, his grateful spirit is revealed. Specifically, there are four reasons for David being grateful in his spirit towards God outlined in this Psalm.

First, David was grateful because it was **the right thing** to do. This is evidenced right away in the first two verses.

Praise the LORD, O my soul; all my inmost being, praise his holy name. Praise the LORD, O my soul, and forget not all his benefits. (Psalm 103:1,2)

Now there is an observation that is interesting to note here. Both phrases *praise the Lord* and *forget not all his benefits* are found in command form in the Hebrew language. They are not mere statements of fact; they are not mere suggestions; but they are commandments to be obeyed. David writing in this way shows that he understood gratitude to be one of his duties to the Lord.

To praise the Lord and to remember God's blessings were both commandments to be obeyed for David.

It is important for each of us to realize that God is the giver of all the good gifts that we have in life. One of the central duties of people given throughout the Bible is to be grateful to God for life and for all that we possess. Gratitude on our part is just common courtesy in response to the many gifts that God has graciously given to us. Most of us instinctively know this in our hearts. This is one reason for a grateful person feeling better and an ungrateful person feeling miserable. Often, our overall satisfaction with ourselves is linked to our faithfulness in discharging our duties. We all have recognized responsibilities and we frankly feel better about ourselves when we faithfully dispatch those duties than when we neglect them.

Most parents can immediately tell what kind of day a child has had at school when the child walks into the house in the afternoon. If the student has finished all his work and behaved himself, then he usually walks in with a cheery smile, eager to show some of his school papers with stars and good grades. On the other hand, if the student has not finished his work and has gotten into trouble at school, he slinks into the house and the parent knows to ask, *what happened at school today?* A student usually feels better knowing that he has successfully performed his duties at school.

That pattern continues with us right through life. There are few better feelings than the satisfied weariness at the end of the day when we have accomplished what we set out to do. But we are generally frustrated when we conclude a day in which few things have gone right and we did not get our duties done. The accomplishment of work naturally brings with it a measure of personal satisfaction.

Many people are not at peace with themselves in the spiritual realm because they do not feel confident that they are fulfilling their spiritual responsibilities before God. Frankly, if we are not maintaining a thankful spirit, we cannot have complete spiritual contentment. The reason for this is the simple fact that gratitude towards God is a duty that we have. It is a commandment given in the Scriptures for us to obey. It is not an option; it is rather a spiritual responsibility. The Apostle Paul wrote to the church at Thessalonica: *Give thanks in all circumstances, for this is God's will for you in Christ Jesus. (1 Thess. 5:18)*

David's use of the command voice here indicates that he realized the importance of this truth, even though he lived hundreds of years before Paul penned those words.

David was also **grateful because of all that God had done for him** and given to him. David's gratitude was not just a grudging sense of duty; it was rather a natural response to all that God had done for him.

Praise the LORD, O my soul, and forget not all his benefits -- who forgives all your sins and heals all your diseases, who redeems your life from the pit and crowns you with love and compassion, who satisfies your desires with good things so that your youth is renewed like the eagle's. The LORD works righteousness and justice for all the oppressed. He made known his ways to Moses, his deeds to the people of Israel. (Psalm 103:2-7)

David wasn't saying *thanks* to God just because he had to but he was rather expressing his gratitude to God from a heart that was overflowing with praise for all that God had done for him.

David gloried in the blessing of forgiveness of sins. What a wonderful, priceless gift this is from God. God sent his one and only Son, the Lord Jesus Christ, to die upon the cross of Calvary so that we might know forgiveness of sins. God's forgiveness is complete. David would later expand this thought by saying, *as far as the east is from the west, so far has he removed our transgressions from us. (Psalm 103:12)* Notice David did not say *as far as the north is from the south* because that would limit God's forgiveness. A person can only travel so far north until the North Pole is crossed and he begins heading south. But it is different traveling east or west. One can begin travelling east and can continue to go around and around the globe always traveling east forever. There are no east or west poles. That is how great God's forgiveness has been towards us. If we have trusted in the Lord Jesus Christ and received this priceless gift of grace from God, God has removed our sins to be remembered against us no more.

David went on to mention the gift of physical health and healing. God is ultimately the giver of health. While we certainly appreciate the many medical advances that have added so much to the quality of our lives and the medical personnel who have dedicated themselves to helping others through physical difficulties, only God can heal the body. Doctors can cut out tumors, sew up incisions, and prescribe medication to fight infections, but only God himself can bring about healing.

The blessings of deliverance from life's dangers and the intangible blessings of love and compassion are also priceless gifts from God. What would the world be like if there were no love or compassion? Have you ever thought about that? Who would want to live in a world that was completely filled with hatred, where there was no love or compassion. Again, God ultimately is the author of these priceless gifts. We have the ability to love because *he first loved us* and created us with the capacity to love one another. *(1 John 4:19)*

James wrote that every good gift that we have ultimately comes from above. *(James 1:17)* The Apostle Paul wrote to Timothy, *for everything that God created is good, and nothing is to be rejected if it is received with thanksgiving. (1 Timothy 4:4)*

Just think for a moment of all of God gifts that we really don't need in order to survive. Now we need food, water, and shelter to survive and God has promised to supply those needs for his children. But think for a moment of all that we have that falls into a category beyond those bare necessities. The appliances that bring such ease to our lives, the transportation that gives us such mobility, the many items for entertainment and recreation, each one a gift that God has given to us.

Justice is also a wonderful gift from God. We often complain about the abuses and injustices in the world, and there are many that could be mentioned. But what if there weren't any standard of justice at all? What kind of a world would that be in which to live? God is the reason for any justice that we have at all. He is a just and righteous God, and he has created us in his image with an inner sense of right and wrong. What a blessing justice is to us.

David so appreciated God's revelation to us. He has made known his ways through Moses and the prophets. What a privilege it is to have God's revelation to us. What would we do in life without His Word? What if we didn't know what God expected of us and had to just guess at what was pleasing to him? But God has not left us without His truth. Over a period of some fifteen hundred years, using more than forty human authors, God carefully and progressively has given his truth to us.

Are you happy for forgiveness of sins, for health, for love and compassion, for every good thing you possess, for justice and righteousness in the world, and for the Scriptures? I certainly am. We should always be ready to say *thanks* to God because he has given all of these benefits to us.

But there was also a third reason for David's grateful spirit. As David had grown in his knowledge of the Lord, he had become more and more **grateful just for who God was.**

The LORD is compassionate and gracious, slow to anger, abounding in love. He will not always accuse, nor will he harbor his anger forever; he does not treat us as our sins deserve or repay us according to our iniquities. For as high as the heavens are above the earth, so great is his love for those who fear him; as far as the east is from the west, so far has he removed our transgressions from us. (Psalm 103:8-12)

God is compassionate and gracious. He is full of mercy and grace. Mercy is God not giving us what we deserve; grace is God giving us what we don't deserve. We deserve God's wrath and judgment for we all have sinned and fallen short of the glory of God. God poured out his righteous wrath on his one and only Son, the Lord Jesus Christ, so that we could be spared. God's compassionate mercy is not giving us what we really deserve. But God didn't stop there. As we are born again into God's family, we are justified, declared to be righteous in God's sight. God made the Lord Jesus Christ to become sin for us, so that we might be made the righteousness of God in him. *(2 Corinthians 5:21)* That's grace! God delights in giving us wonderful blessings that we don't deserve.

God is patient. He is slow to anger. He abounds in love. Patience is such a key virtue in life. Someone defined patience as the ability to throttle your motor when you feel like stripping your gears. If we have trouble with impatience with the small, seemingly insignificant plans that we have, just think of how wonderful it is that God is patient. After all, God has designed the perfect plan for the universe. But he is patient, willing to work out this plan in his own perfect timing. A farmer will never reap the fruit if he plucks the blossoms. God is a patient God, waiting for the fruit to be born in its season.

And God is loving. He is not vengeful or vindictive. Someone made the observation that *love looks through a telescope; envy through a microscope.* Just think of what life would be like if an infinitely perfect God stood watching over us with the attitude of immediately correcting every single one of our mistakes, no matter how minor. Life would be intolerable. Aren't you happy that God is a God of love? Love covers a multitude of sins. Just think of what this world would be like if the Devil were god? Just think of the horror that we would experience if Satan were able to execute his vile character with omnipotence? God delights in providing atonement for his people so that the guilt and shame of their sins might be covered.

When we consider the source of David's thoughts here, the message becomes even more profound. Part of the statement that David quoted here, reflecting upon the character of God, was taken directly from Exodus 34 in a statement given by God about himself. As Moses was going up the mount to receive the law for the second time, having chiseled out two new tablets of stone, the Bible records in Exodus 34:6, *And God passed in front of Moses, proclaiming, "The Lord, the Lord, the compassionate and gracious God, slow to anger, abounding in love and faithfulness."*

When we consider the historical situation of this quotation that David used in this Psalm, the wonderful character of God becomes even more pronounced. God had redeemed his people from the bondage of Egyptian slavery. With a mighty hand, he had brought them forth out of Egypt, then the most powerful nation on earth. The Israelites had even walked out of Egypt, laden down with great riches that the Egyptians had freely given to them. This was something unheard of in human history. God had brought them to the foot of Mt. Sinai in order to give to them his law, his revelation that reflected his character. But then, as Moses tarried in the presence of a patient God near the top of Mt. Sinai, these impatient Israelites had the nerve to make another god out of gold. They had formed a golden calf and were worshiping it. Imagine that! They had used the very gold that God had moved the Egyptian people to give as an added blessing to make another god to worship. This was the gold that God planned to use for the sacred articles of his holy tabernacle. What would you have done to the Israelites if you had been god? Do you know what God did? He demonstrated his compassion and mercy towards his people by forgiving even this great atrocity and affront to his holy character. And as Moses came up to that mountain the second time, with this example fresh in his mind, God revealed himself as the compassionate and gracious God, slow to anger, and abounding in love. David was thankful for the character and attributes of God. And the more we get to know God, the more thankful we become for the magnificence of his infinite being.

David was also grateful for the relationship that he had with the Lord.

As a father has compassion on his children, so the LORD has compassion on those who fear him; for he knows

how we are formed, he remembers that we are dust.
(Psalm 103:13,14)

Just as a model earthly father has compassion on his children and uses his strength and wisdom for their benefit, so God loves his children and has made all of his unlimited resources available to them. We don't have to journey through this life in the strength of our own flesh. We are just animated dust. There is no strength really there. We were formed from the union of two cells and every one of our physical bodies will return back to dust one day. But the good news is that every believer has a Heavenly Father who knows exactly who we are and loves us anyway. Every believer has a Heavenly Father who has committed all of his unlimited resources to the welfare, protection and growth of his children. We can be thankful for that!

In this Psalm, David has built **a stair-like progression** that is reflected in the heart of a person with a grateful spirit.

Often, gratitude, as with other Christian virtues, starts because of a sense of duty. The Christian who desires with all of his heart to walk in integrity before the Lord submits himself to obey God with an undivided heart.

But then, as one grows just a little bit in the Lord, and as he begins to experience the many blessings that God generously bestows upon his children, he is led to be grateful to God in response to all of the benefits that God provides.

And as a person grows in his knowledge of God and learns more and more about him, he then begins to realize the awesome character of a God who alone is worthy of all praise, adoration and worship. The Christian is moved to be grateful to God just for who he is apart from a sense of duty or any of the gifts that he gives.

But then the final and highest level of thanksgiving comes. As we grow in our relationship with God so that we experience the intimacy of a Heavenly Father, and as we walk in daily fellowship with this One who has become our very life, we are then led to live the grateful life that God intended for us. This is a life that fills our hearts with joy, peace and contentment. This is the life that makes any other type of living just a shadow in comparison.

David knew this kind of living. That is what made him *a man after God's own heart*. And each of us can know this type of life as well. For God is great enough to have the most intimate relationship with every single one of his children.

A LIVING LORD
Chapter 18

In his book entitled *Through the Wilderness of Loneliness,* Tim Hansel tells a moving story about a young boy named Johnny. Johnny was an elementary-aged student with a terminal illness. His disease made it difficult for him to understand school assignments. But his teacher and fellow classmates realized that it was best for Johnny to live as normal a life as he could for as long as he could so they just overlooked Johnny's miscues in class.

It was during the Easter season that the teacher thought of an idea for a way to affirm each of the students in her classroom. She instructed them to bring in an empty Legg's pantyhose container that, of course, is in the shape of an Easter egg. The students were to put something inside the eggs that reminded them of Easter or life. She then planned to take each egg in turn, open it and make some positive comments about what was contained inside, affirming each of her students.

As she opened egg after egg and saw the faces of her students brighten up, the instructor knew that this had been a worthy project and she made a mental note to put it in her lesson plan again in future years. But then she came to Johnny's egg. When she opened it up, she found it to be empty. Assuming that Johnny just hadn't understood the assignment and not wanting to embarrass him publicly, she just continued on to the next egg until she had finished with the entire class. But she was unable to move on to the next project in her lesson plan gracefully because Johnny raised his hand.

Teacher, you didn't share my egg, Johnny protested.

I know, Johnny, and I'm sorry, his teacher answered back. *But evidently you didn't understand the assignment. You were supposed to put something in the egg that reminds you of life or Easter.*

I know, continued Johnny. *When the women came to Jesus' tomb on Sunday morning, it was empty. That's really what life is all about, isn't it? Because his grave was empty, we know that we can live again after we die.*

Only then did the teacher realize that in his simplicity Johnny had captured the Easter message more than any other student. It was just a few weeks later that his fellow students noticed Johnny's desk was empty. Johnny had gone to the hospital. Within a few days, he passed away. As friends of the family visited the funeral home to pay their respects, they noticed something that was most unusual. In Johnny's little casket, his classmates had placed twenty-seven empty Legg's pantyhose eggs. Johnny's testimony had come through loud and clear.

There is no symbol that more completely sums up the meaning of this life than that empty tomb that those first women and then John and Peter found in the garden. For the easiest way to distort this life and make it lose all of its meaning is to make this life an end in itself. Anyone who lives totally for this earthly life finds it to be empty and void of true significance.

There is no pleasure or luxury that this world can offer that can bring lasting satisfaction. One of the paradoxes of this life is found in the fact that a person only finds the true meaning of life as he realizes that this life has been designed to prepare us for an eternal life to follow. This life is the trial run; this life is the dress rehearsal; the real life, the feature presentation comes only after we die.

We see this truth pictured in the Living Lord that we worship. The quality of the life of Jesus on this earth was mediocre at best and downright miserable at worst. Christ's life had its enjoyable moments. He built some lasting relationships with his disciples and had some good times of fellowship with them. But when one compares that to the poverty in which he lived and the rejections that he received and the pain and torture that he suffered, few would choose to live that kind of life if given the choice. But the glorious truth of the overall picture is that the Lord Jesus Christ returned to live his glorious existence after he died. For it was his resurrection from the dead that ushered him into fullness of life once again.

Psalm 110 speaks of the relationship that David had with the Living Lord. In this Psalm, David spoke prophetically of three glorious ministries that the Lord Jesus Christ has as our Risen Savior. We know beyond a shadow of a doubt that David is writing this Psalm prophetically of the Lord Jesus because he begins by saying, *The LORD says to my Lord.*

The LORD says to my Lord: "Sit at my right hand

235

until I make your enemies a footstool for your feet."
(Psalm 110:1)

There are two different Hebrew words that are used here for Lord. The first, *Jehovah* or *Yahweh*, is the most sacred term for God in the Old Testament. There can be no question that David is referring to Almighty God when he first says *Lord*. The second, *adonai*, literally means *master* or *owner*. It is also a common term for deity in the Old Testament, but it is often used of human beings who were in a position of power as well. But we know that David could not be using this term of a mere human because David was now King as he wrote these words. There wasn't any human being who could be called his lord, his master. So it is obvious that David is speaking in a prophetic sense of his divine owner, his Creator, the Lord Jesus Christ who would come to earth as God's Messiah. If we would have need of any further confirmation that this Psalm is prophetic, the Lord Jesus himself gave that when he used this very passage in reference to himself confounding the wisest rabbis of his day as recorded in each of the synoptic gospels *(Matthew 22:44; Mark 12:36; Luke 20:42)*. So there can be no question that in writing this Psalm, David is looking forward to the coming of the Messiah.

Now there are **three pictures** of the Living Lord that are presented in this Psalm. Each of these was also significant in the life of King David.

The first picture is the **victorious warrior**.

The LORD says to my Lord: "Sit at my right hand until I make your enemies a footstool for your feet." The LORD will extend your mighty scepter from Zion; you will rule in the midst of your enemies. Your troops will be willing on your day of battle. Arrayed in holy majesty, from the womb of the dawn you will receive the dew of your youth.

There is certainly a sense in which these verses were fulfilled in the life of David for God's plan was to give King David a great and mighty kingdom. God's plan was for David to exercise control over most of the countries of the Middle East by the end of his reign. In fact, Israel never had before David, nor has it ever had since, the dominance that it enjoyed during the reign of King David. From Egypt in the south to Syria in the north, from the Mediterranean Sea on the West past the lands of Moab, Edom and Ammon to the east of the Jordan River, all of this area was controlled by King David by the end of his reign. David was certainly a great military leader. There is not a battle recorded in the Bible where David was the loser.

But in studying this Psalm, there is also the realization that the ultimate fulfillment must come with God's Messiah. This picture of the victorious warrior is ultimately fulfilled after Christ's resurrection, for Jesus did not come to be a conquering king the first time, but he rather came as the suffering servant. Christ did not attempt a coup of the Roman government; he did not try to organize zealots into a united force; he did not stir up the people with revolutionary speeches. Rather he presented God's truths of personal peace; he taught that the kingdom of God was within a person; he told his followers that in order to be great, they must be servants to all.

In fact, the Lord Jesus looked to be anything but the conquering victor as he was hanging helplessly upon Calvary's cross. It appeared that God's enemy had finally gained the victory. The forces of evil were celebrating during that time when darkness enveloped the earth.

But those days of rejoicing for God's enemies were short-lived. For when the Lord Jesus rose in triumph from the grave, another chapter had been written in God's redemptive book. Before, the frail body of Jesus had succumbed to physical death, but now the resurrected body of Christ had gained victory over the grave. Before, nails driven by Roman soldiers held Jesus' body to that wooden cross, but now the resurrected body of Christ could move from place to place instantaneously and walk through doors and walls. Before, Jesus was subject to the cruel whims of his creatures, but now the resurrected Christ had become the firstfruits of all creation.

There is an ancient Greek legend that illustrates the victory of the Lord Jesus Christ. A young son of the king of Troy named Paris had kidnapped Helen, the beautiful wife of the Menelaus, the king of Sparta. Of course, Menelaus' honor had been defiled and he missed the companionship of his wife. So, the Spartan king joined together all of the forces that he could muster to attack the city of Troy, to rescue his wife Helen. For ten years the armies of Sparta continued to siege the city of Troy to no avail. Troy was just too well-fortified to be taken. Finally, the Greek hero, Ulysses, thought of a way to gain entrance into the city. He had the Spartan soldiers construct a large, hollow horse. When it was completed, as many Greek soldiers as could fit were sealed inside the horse's belly. The huge horse was then left outside the city gate and the remaining Greek soldiers boarded their ships and sailed around the corner of the peninsula, out of sight.

The citizens of Troy were baffled by this change in strategy at first. After ten years of steady siege, they didn't know what to make of the abrupt departure of the Spartan soldiers and this huge, wooden horse left behind. But they finally decided that the Greek soldiers had given up their fight, returning to their native land, and that they had left this horse as an offering to the goddess, Athena, so that they might have safety on their trip. Not wanting to risk the disfavor of Athena, Paris led his men to wheel the huge horse into the walls of the city. Then the Trojans began to party; their victory had finally been secured.

Little did they know that while they were getting themselves into a drunken stupor, the Greek ships were turning around and returning back into the Trojan harbor. And in the night, the secluded soldiers inside the horse's belly opened a secret trap door, dropped to the ground and opened the gates of the city to a waiting army of Spartan soldiers. In one night, the Spartan army was able to accomplish what they hadn't been able to do for a decade. The city of Troy was defeated, burned to the ground and Queen Helen was rescued and taken back to Sparta.

As the Lord Jesus Christ hung upon that Roman cross of execution, the Devil thought that he had finally won the victory. He had captured the minds and hearts of the creatures that God had created for fellowship and now he thought that he would have them forever. We can only imagine the celebration that was going on in the spiritual realm of darkness as the Son of God was being put to death.

But just when Satan thought that he had gained the final victory, the Lord Jesus Christ suddenly rose from the tomb with divine power. He rose to free his people from spiritual bondage. In one dramatic event, Satan was defeated forever.

There is coming a day when the Lord Jesus Christ will return as the conquering victor. He will appear in the skies, riding his white horse with all of the heavenly armies at his side according to Revelation 19. There will be a great battle on that day, the battle that we call Armageddon. But the outcome of that battle has already been assured. It was assured by the events that took place at the end of Christ's first coming. For when Jesus died on the cross and rose from the grave, Satan was defeated finally and forever.

The second picture of the Living Lord that is found in this Psalm is the **continuing priest**.

*The LORD has sworn and will not change his mind:
"You are a priest forever, in the order of Melchizedek."
(Psalm 110:4)*

Now as King, David didn't actually function as a priest offering sacrifices, but he did represent his people before God like a priest would. And David was the one who initiated bringing the Ark of the Covenant back to its rightful place. But it is clear in this Psalm that David was again writing prophetically for he spoke of an obscure priest named Melchizedek.

The priest was the person in the Old Testament who represented the people to God. In order to be a priest for the nation of Israel, a person had to come from the tribe of Levi. The High Priest was always the direct descendent from Aaron. Each priest performed his years of ministry for the people and then he died, leaving his function to the next generation to carry on.

But there was another priest who mysteriously appeared long before Aaron was even born or Moses wrote out the ceremonial functions in the law. His name was Melchizedek. He was a priest for God in the city of Peace, Salem. This city today is called Jerusalem which means *city of peace*. Almost nothing is known about this man, Melchizedek.   He suddenly appears in the fourteenth chapter of Genesis.

*After Abram returned from defeating Kedorlaomer
and the kings allied with him, the king of Sodom came out*

to meet him in the Valley of Shaveh (that is, the King's Valley).

Then Melchizedek king of Salem brought out bread and wine. He was priest of God Most High, and he blessed Abram, saying, "Blessed be Abram by God Most High, Creator of heaven and earth. And blessed be God Most High, who delivered your enemies into your hand."

Then Abram gave him a tenth of everything. (Genesis 14:17-20)

Melchizedek blessed Abraham after he returned from his victorious battle, received tithes from the patriarch, blessed the great man of faith and then disappeared back into the realm of anonymity. No date of birth or account of death is given for Melchizedek. No genealogy or ancestry is given of him. Because of his sudden and mysterious appearance, some theologians feel that Melchizedek was actually an appearance of the Lord Jesus Christ in a pre-incarnate form. We can't be dogmatic about this for we just don't have enough information. But we do know that Melchizedek becomes an important figure for he pictures the priesthood of the Lord Jesus Christ in contrast to Aaron's priesthood. Jesus was a priest after the order of Melchizedek, not after the order of Aaron.

The author of Hebrews devoted several chapters to develop the significance of the Messiah's priesthood. Aaron and the priests who followed him were mere men who were born, lived and died. By not having any record of his birth or death, Melchizedek became a symbol of one who is eternal, who had no beginning and will never die. Aaron and the priests who followed him had to first offer sacrifices for their own sins before they interceded on the behalf of others. There is no record of Melchizedek offering any sacrifices for himself, nor did Jesus offer a sacrifice for himself because he was the sinless Lamb of God. Christ's sacrifice was for others. Aaron and the priests who followed him had to continuously offer sacrifices year after year proving that the sacrifices themselves were not sufficient to fully pay for sins. But the Lord Jesus Christ after the order of Melchizedek offered only one sacrifice. This sacrifice was himself and it was sufficient to totally pay for sin.

Now the beautiful truth that David brought out in this Psalm was that Jesus, being a priest after the order of Melchizedek, continues in that priestly ministry forever. The sacrifice has been paid once for all. When the Lord Jesus Christ said *it is finished* from the cross, our sins were paid in full. But even now, seated at the right hand of God, the Lord Jesus continues the intercessory ministry of a priest on our behalf. The author of Hebrews wrote these words that bring such strength and comfort to our hearts.

For we do not have a high priest who is unable to sympathize with our weaknesses, but we have one who has been tempted in every way, just as we are - yet was without sin. Let us then approach the throne of grace with confidence, so that we may receive mercy and find grace to help us in our time of need. (Hebrews 4:15,16)

Because the Lord Jesus Christ is the Living Lord, we will never have a need for another priest again. We will also have one to intercede on our behalf before God the Father. For Jesus Christ is a priest forever; he is an ever-living priest.

The Lord Jesus Christ as the Living Lord is not only a victorious warrior and an eternal priest, but he is also the **righteous judge**.

He will judge the nations. (Psalm 110:6)

Part of David's job as king was to provide an example of justice for his people. But he recognized that there was another ruler and judge to whom he answered, one who was far more powerful that he. One of the most important truths that is taught in the Scriptures is the fact that one day every single person will stand before the Lord Jesus Christ and give an account of his or her life.

Jesus Christ is the creator of all things; by him were all things created, Colossians 1:16 says. Jesus Christ is the sustainer of all things; by his powerful word all things are presently being held together, Hebrews 1:3 says. So everything that exists is accountable to the creator and sustainer. And the Bible says that one day everyone will stand before the righteous judge to give an account of his or her life.

For we must all appear before the judgment seat of Christ, that each one may receive what is due him for the things done while in the body, whether good or bad. (2 Corinthians 5:10)

A judgment seat can be a place of excited anticipation or dreaded terror depending upon what is received. The Olympic athlete who has won his or her event can't wait to get to the judgment seat so that the gold medal might be received. But the student who is sent to the principal's office because of misbehavior walks that long hallway with fearful anticipation.

God has given to us all that we need to be prepared to come to the judgment seat of Christ with excited anticipation. God sent his one and only Son into the world to pay the penalty for our sins. God promises to make all of those who confess their sins and receive his forgiveness through the Lord Jesus Christ members of his own divine family.

So those who are children of God will be welcomed home at the judgment seat of Christ. They will finally be home in heaven with God for all eternity. They will be rewarded for service rendered for the Lord here in this life. We can have this confidence and assurance because we worship a Living Lord.